JAPANESE BASEBALL

JAPANESE BASEBALL

A Fan's Guide

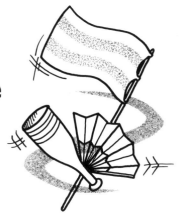

Brian Maitland

Charles E. Tuttle Company
Rutland, Vermont & Tokyo, Japan

Line drawings by Jude Brand

Published by the Charles E. Tuttle Co., Inc.
of Rutland, Vermont & Tokyo, Japan
with editorial offices
at 2-6 Suido 1-chome, Bunkyo-ku, Tokyo 112

LCC Card No. 91-65062
ISBN 0-8048-1680-8

First edition, 1991

Printed in Japan

CONTENTS

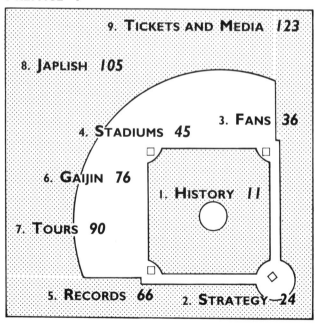

NOTE:

Western name order, i.e., given name followed by surname, has been used throughout the book. Macrons, signifying long vowels in romanized Japanese, have been retained only with italicized words within the text.

PREFACE

FROM CANADA to Venezuela, from Cuba to Taiwan, baseball is a sport that has been embraced by many cultures. But nowhere are culture and baseball more intertwined than in Japan. Call it the national pastime in America but in Japan baseball is more a national religion.

Sports anywhere are an insight into culture, be it soccer in Brazil, hockey in Canada, or rugby in New Zealand. And despite the spoutings of purists who want to keep sports separate from politics or culture, it is undeniable that sports absorb and reflect aspects of the society around them, both the good and the bad. This is why attending a professional baseball game is one of the best ways to gain a fresh insight into the often-analyzed country called Japan.

Baseball in Japan is played at a different pace, in a different style, and with different strategies than the game many of us grew up with. One comment you're bound to hear is that Japanese professional baseball is not as good as Major League ball. Given that marginal Major Leaguers can become big stars here, it is true that the level of play seems to be a step below Major League level. In fact, Japanese professional baseball tends to be of minor-league AAA level, a significant difference being that the Japanese play in Major League-capacity stadiums.

But baseball is baseball, wherever you go, whatever the game. If you're a real fan, you'll watch sandlot ball, the Little League World Series, the Olympics, etc. Japanese professional baseball is yet another demonstration of the long established sport, well worth investigating by both serious and not-so-serious fans. And even if you're not a fan at all, you can still enjoy the trappings of Japanese baseball: the colorful cheering sections, the bizarre selection of food ("Get your *udon* and curry rice here!"), the advertising blitz of stadium billboards, the plain curiosity of 50,000 people sitting in one spot watching a man try to hit a ball with a stick.

To put it simply, you'll have FUN at a Japanese ballgame. Whether it's a tension-filled duel between two top clubs or a relaxed encounter between the lesser lights, baseball has something for everybody. A game can be a chance to relax and get away from the stress of everyday life, or it can be a time to let off steam and cheer your favorite team to victory.

An added bonus of a Japanese baseball game is the people-watching. The ballpark is one place where you'll see Japanese let down their guard, revealing their feelings for a game they like as passionately as any fan across the pond does. At a ballgame the stereotypical shyness and reserved nature of the Japanese are simply not in evidence. The sheer noise level (paralleling college-sports enthusiasm in the U.S.) should prove there's a link between behavior and environment. Put any people on the sporting stage and out comes their true character, the one suppressed at the office, at home, at school.

By touring Japan's ballparks you'll learn how each team has its own identity and outlook, shown not only by the players but reflected in the fans and the city itself. Even if you can't make it to the ballpark, watch a game on TV and you'll be surprised at what you see. Behind the superficial sameness of a supposedly homogeneous culture lie those quirks that make up the psyche of the Japanese whole. And Japanese baseball is full of the quirks that make life here interesting for resident and tourist alike.

I would like to thank Hiromi Isoda, Nob and Kako, Ken Chow, Wayne Graczyk, and Walter Long for their various contributions to this project. The book could not have been completed without their generous and valuable assistance. Any errors within the book are my responsibility alone.

Brian Maitland

Tokyo, Japan

I

HISTORY

THE YAKULT SWALLOWS are playing the Chunichi Dragons on television tonight. You haul out your Rand McNally *Concise World Atlas* but can't seem to find the fine cities of Yakult and Chunichi on the map of Japan. It says "professional baseball" in tonight's TV listings but what cities are being represented here? Therein lies Japanese baseball's reflection of the culture from which it sprung.

Since ancient times, people have picked up pieces of wood, tossed spherical objects at each other, and called it sport. Perpetuating this activity required capital to build stadiums and pay participants. Early Neanderthal man may have first crossed the ice floes in search of corporate sponsors for his sport. The practice continues today, particularly in Japan, where professional baseball is totally dependent upon direct corporate sponsorship of teams. So it's not the Nagoya Dragons you're about to watch but the Dragons sponsored by the Chunichi newspaper group; the rival Swallows, based in Tokyo, are sponsored by the Yakult health-drink company.

All professional baseball teams in Japan are directly sponsored by a corporation. And it is the corporation's wealth and power that account for the success or failure of the sports team. Of course, sports around the world are really not that much different. Sponsors' logos emblazon European soccer clubs' uniforms, and logos cover Formula One race cars. The Japanese have simply taken the next logical step and added the company name to the team name. Be it the Fuji Film volleyball squad, the Nissan soccer club, or the Chunichi Dragons, all Japanese sports teams at the pro and semipro level are corporately sponsored and labeled. Like North American cities that aim to get on the sports map to further civic pride and increase business at local hotels and restaurants, Japanese corporations have embraced sports for similar not-so-sporting aims. The Japanese corporation hopes daily exposure of the company name on TV and in the sports pages will pay off in its corporate ventures, be it sales of Chunichi newspapers or Yakult health drinks.

Although it might be hard for North Americans to get revved up and cheer for, say, the Domino's Pizza Tigers instead of the Detroit Tigers (Tigers' owner Tom Monaghan is the founder of Domino's Pizza), Japanese tend to take their teams' corporate ties in stride. The names may be corporately based but civic pride still lies at the core. The Dragons may be a branch of the Chunichi newspaper group but to their home fans in Nagoya, the Chunichi Dragons represent their city, regardless of the team's name.

People especially identify with a city or a corporation if it produces a winning team. And the biggest winner in the history of Japanese baseball is that most corporate of all teams, the Yomiuri Giants of Tokyo. Formed in 1934 as the first fully professional baseball club in the land, the Giants (Kyojin in Japanese) have long dominated Japanese pro baseball both on the field and at the box office. The Yomiuri group has its own television station, NTV (Nippon Television), which broadcasts the Giants' entire home schedule. The Yomiuri newspaper, which has the highest circulation in the world, reaches out to praise the Giants every day and night of the year. With this powerful media onslaught, it's no wonder that generation after generation the Giants have remained the most popular team in Japan.

The Giants average over 45,000 people for every home game they play. On the road, they are such a good drawing card that some clubs raise ticket prices to cash in on their popularity. Though the Giants are based in Tokyo, there are Giants' fans in every corner of Japan, ensuring huge crowds of support at all road games.

For the other corporations in the Japanese baseball market it's an uphill battle. The Central League's other teams lack the financial muscle to compete consistently with the Yomiuri corporate steamroller. Perhaps trying hardest are the Hanshin Tigers, sponsored by the Hanshin railway company of Osaka, but the Tigers perennially seem to play second fiddle to the Giants' successes in much the same way that Osaka lies in Tokyo's shadow. The other Central League clubs win an occasional pennant but over decades of play the Giants have prevailed.

Backed by Toyo Kogyo, the parent group of Mazda Motors, the Hiroshima Toyo Carp have managed to field some strong teams. The Yokohama Taiyo Whales, sponsored by the Taiyo fish-packing company, have not been as successful, but the team's name seems appropriate for this famous port city. The other two teams in the

Central League, the Chunichi Dragons and the Yakult Swallows, benefit from having the Giants in their league. Meanwhile, the Pacific League suffers due to the Giants' absence.

The Pacific League's current corporate leader is the Seibu Lions. Sponsored by the Seibu Ryutsu group, whose railway links Tokyo with the Lions' home stadium in Saitama prefecture, the Seibu Lions too have become both champions at the box office and on the field. With huge financial reserves at their disposal, the Lions have managed to secure a prominent place in the Tokyo baseball market in a relatively short time. Seibu department stores located throughout Tokyo present a high profile for the club, as do the sales that follow Lions' pennant victories. A very visible corporate image that speaks of being in touch with the latest trends and aims at the youth of Tokyo has been very successful for Seibu. Playing in Tokorozawa in Saitama prefecture (a 40-minute train ride from central Tokyo), the Lions are a Tokyo club in all but the location of their stadium.

Despite being in the area longer than the Lions, the other Tokyo-area Pacific League clubs have not garnered the support that Seibu has. The Nippon Ham Fighters, sponsored by the Nippon Ham meat-packaging company, are overshadowed by the Giants, with whom they share Tokyo Dome. The Lotte Orions of Kawasaki are sponsored by a Korean firm, the Lotte confectionary company, which produces the Lotte gum and chocolate seen at every corner store in Japan. As visible as its products are, the Lotte group spends little money on the Kawasaki team. Instead, the Lotte Giants of the Korean baseball league get priority in Lotte's world of corporate baseball sponsorship, leaving the Lotte Orions of the Japanese league as poor cousins.

In Osaka the Kintetsu Buffaloes are sponsored by the Kintetsu Railway company, while the Orix BlueWave is sponsored by Orient Leasing, in essence a shipping company. Further west, in Fukuoka on the island of Kyushu, are the Daiei Hawks, owned by the Daiei supermarket chain.

The previous paragraphs describe how Japan's corporate baseball world stands at present. However, teams have often moved or changed owners, changed names, mascots, etc. The entire history of the shifts and swings of Japan's professional baseball teams is a checkered one.

Central League

Yomiuri Giants 1947–present
Tokyo Kyojin 1934–46

Hiroshima Toyo Carp 1968–present
Hiroshima Carp 1950–67

Yakult Swallows 1974–present
Yakult Atoms 1970–73
Atoms 1969
Sankei Atoms 1966–68
Sankei Swallows 1965
Kokutetsu Swallows 1950–64

Chunichi Dragons 1953–present
Nagoya Dragons 1951–52
Chunichi Dragons 1948–50
Chubu Nippon Dragons 1947
Chubu Nippon 1946
Sangyo 1944
Nagoya 1936–43

Hanshin Tigers 1961–present
Osaka Tigers 1946–60
Hanshin 1940–44
Osaka Tigers 1935–39

Yokohama Taiyo Whales 1978–present
Taiyo Whales 1955–77
Taiyo Shochiku Robins 1953–54[1]

Pacific League

Seibu Lions 1979–present
Crown Lighter Lions 1977–78
Taiheiyo Club Lions 1973–76
Nishitetsu Lions 1951–72[2]

Nippon Ham Fighters 1974–present
Nittaku Home Flyers 1973
Toei Flyers 1954–72
Tokyu Flyers 1949–53
Kyuei Flyers 1948
Tokyu Flyers 1947
Senators 1946

Orix BlueWave 1991–present
Orix Braves 1989–90

1. The Taiyo Shochiku Robins were formed when the Taiyo Whales (1950–52) merged with the Shochiku Robins (1950–52). The Shochiku Robins had gone through a number of evolutions: Daiyo Robins (1948–49), Taiyo Robins (1947), Pacific (1946), Asahi (1941–44), Lion (1937–40), Dai Tokyo (1936).
2. The Nishitetsu Lions were formed when the Nishitetsu Clippers (1950) merged with the Nishi-Nippon Pirates (1950).

Hankyu Braves 1947–88
Hankyu 1936–46

Kintetsu Buffaloes 1962–present
Kintetsu Buffalo 1959–61
Kintetsu Pearls 1950–58

Fukuoka Daiei Hawks 1989–present
Nankai Hawks 1947–88
Kinki Great Ring 1946
Kinki Nihon 1944
Nankai 1938–43

Lotte Orions 1969–present
Tokyo Orions 1964–68
Daimai Orions 1958–63[3]

Due to the Allies' impending advance on Japan toward
the end of World War II, the baseball season was suspended in 1945. Play resumed in 1946 but without two
clubs, Nishitetsu and Daiwa, which had disbanded.

Nishitetsu 1943
Taiyo 1941–42[4]

3. The Daimai Orions were formed when the Mainichi Orions
(1950–57) merged with the Daiei Unions (1957). The Daiei
Unions were formed when the Daiei Stars (1949–56) merged with
the Takahashi Unions (1956). The Daiei Stars were previously
the Kinsei Stars (1947–48) and Grandstar (1946). The Takahashi
Unions were previously the Tombo Unions (1955) and the Takahashi Unions (1954).

4. Taiyo was formed when Nagoya Kinko (1936–40) merged with
Tsubasa (1940). Tsubasa was previously the Tokyo Senators
(1936–39).

Daiwa 1942–43
Kurowashi 1940–41
Eagles 1937–39

Organized league play in Japan dates from 1936, when Tokyo Kyojin, the Osaka Tigers, Hankyu, Nagoya Kinko, Nagoya, Dai Tokyo, and the Tokyo Senators fielded teams. That grand first season consisted of three league games and two tournament games. As if an indication of things to come, Kyojin came out on top and the Tigers were runners-up.

The first professional baseball game in Japan took place at Nagoya's Narumi Stadium, pitting Kyojin against Nagoya Kinko. If you search hard enough, you can still find part of this old stadium, as its infield stands form the garage roof of a driver-training center on the same spot in Nagoya.

The 1937 and 1938 seasons were played on a split schedule, with champions crowned in the fall and spring seasons. From 1939 to 1949 (except for 1945), an eight-team league played a full schedule of games. Franchises shifted and owners changed but the basic structure remained the same. Kyojin, with a head start on the competition, laid the foundation for their later success in those early days. During one particularly successful span, they reeled off five pennants in a row.

In 1950 the Central and Pacific Leagues were created, and the total number of clubs expanded from eight to fifteen. After an initial few years that weeded out the weaker members, the Central League got down to its current six clubs in 1953, while the Pacific League rounded off to six clubs in 1958. The two-league system created the need for a contest between the champions of the two leagues. In the first Japan Series in 1950, the Shochiku Robins defeated the Mainichi Orions four games to two.

Over the years the two leagues have developed distinctive brands of baseball in much the same way the National League and American League have developed different styles. The Central League is more bound by tradition; for example, its pitchers still bat in the regular batting order. This strategy may appeal to traditionalists but at times has made for play that is less daring and exciting than that seen in the Pacific League.

Another factor aiding the rise of the Pacific League was the Giants' almost total domination of the Central League from the mid 1960s to the mid 1970s (much like the New York Yankees' domination of the American League from the 1940s to the 1950s). From 1965 to 1973 the Giants won nine straight Central League titles, and the league seemed to polarize around this single club.

To address the imbalance of power, the draft system was introduced in 1965. The order of the draft is determined by the result of the Japan Series. If a Central League team wins the Series, the last-place Pacific League club drafts first, followed by the last-place Central League club. The draft alternates this way up through the standings until the champions take the twelfth and final pick of each round. Each club can select six players only. Unfortunately the draft system has not always worked as intended.

In 1977 Hosei University star pitcher Suguru Egawa was chosen by the Crown Lighter Lions. Egawa, however, determined to play for the Yomiuri Giants, refused to join the Lions and spent the year playing ball in the U.S. He re-entered the draft in November 1978, was chosen by the Hanshin Tigers, but again refused to play for anyone but Yomiuri. The situation was deadlocked until the spring of 1979, when the Giants traded ace pitcher Shigeru Kobayashi to the Tigers for the rights to Egawa. As draft choices cannot be traded, the deal was against baseball rules, stirred considerable controversy, forced the resignation of the baseball commissioner, but Egawa became a Giant. The incident sparked new calls for revision of the draft, and the lottery system was introduced.

The new rules stipulate that if a player is chosen by more than one team, a lottery will determine which team wins the right to sign him. A glaring flaw in the revised system is that weaker teams remain weak if they are not lucky in the lottery. But even winning the lottery does not necessarily mean that a team will sign a particular player. A player disappointed at being drafted by a club not to his liking often refuses to sign a contract. He then sits out the upcoming season and re-enters the draft the following season. In recent years, some clubs have acceded to a reluctant player's wishes and not chosen him a second time, leaving the player free to sign with his favorite team.

As originally set up, the draft took some time to begin to change the power structure of Japanese baseball. In fact, it was in 1965, the year the draft was established, that the Giants began their legendary "V-9," Victory Nine, nine consecutive Central League and Japan Series titles. Despite the flaws of the draft, however, the system has helped redistribute talent. The Giants still win their share of pennants but they no longer dominate Japanese pro baseball the way they did in earlier years.

In particular, the draft has aided the Pacific League, and in the process made the Japan Series a more even battle between the two league champions. From 1950 to 1973 the Giants alone won 15 Japan Series titles, while the Pacific League clubs together took just six. In contrast, between 1974 and 1990 Pacific League teams took ten Japan Series while Central League teams won seven.

Being perceived as the weaker league forced the Pacific League to institute innovations to attract fans away from the more popular Central League. The designated hitter was introduced in 1975, and a split season was tried for a few seasons. For Sunday games, Pacific League starting pitchers are announced in advance, a common practice in the Majors but not in Japan, where managers traditionally keep lineups secret until game time. From cutesy high-school pompom girls to bizarre furry mascots, the Pacific League has tried various ploys to increase popularity. Even the teams' uniforms show a splash of color, from the deep ocean blue of the Orix Blue-Wave to the fluorescent orange of the Nippon Ham Fighters.

The Pacific League routinely features high-scoring games; an eight-run lead in the bottom of the ninth isn't always safe. Such dramatic comebacks occur mainly in home-run parks like the Kintetsu Buffaloes' Fujiidera Stadium and the Lotte Orions' Kawasaki Stadium. However, as recent all-star games have shown, the Pacific League now has better players than the Central League.

The Central League, of course, has its fair share of good players but the two leagues do seem to breed different styles of play. Given the power of Tokyo and Osaka, and those two cities' most popular teams, the Giants and the Tigers, the Central League will always draw well. However, the Pacific League produces the better pennant races, as basically anything can happen and often does happen in a Pacific League game. Perhaps the Pacific League's more competitive pennant races and "try harder" attitude have finally paid off. Or perhaps the concentration of talent in the Giants' hands over so many seasons has dulled the other Central League clubs' competitive edge.

Whatever the reason, the Central League features more systematic and organized play, while the Pacific League provides more exciting baseball. The opposite viewpoint has it that Central League games are more intense thrillers and Pacific League games are looser and lacking in intensity. From the number of spectators, it appears that the Japanese fan prefers the Central League brand of baseball. Or perhaps it is still the Giants' huge drawing power that makes the Central League more popular.

But even the mighty Giants cannot compete with high-school baseball. Despite the year-round popularity of the pro game, for two weeks in summer it takes a back bleacher seat to the high-school tournament held at Koshien Stadium in Nishinomiya, *the* baseball event in Japan.

Over 900,000 people attend the summer tournament that pits teams from each of Japan's 47 prefectures battling for the high-school crown. The highly partisan crowds of high schoolers supporting their teams are the most emotional of all baseball fans in Japan. Tears of sorrow or joy flow as young hopes are dashed or raised. The all-white uniforms and closely cropped hair of the players, backed up by high schoolers in military-type uniforms rooting in the stands, combine to add a surreal touch to the popular event.

The high-school tournament, begun in 1924, is Japanese baseball's link to its true roots. The spectacle of youthful innocence somehow mythicizes the whole affair. Also, the commonly shared experience of high school makes for a very nostalgic memory for almost all Japanese. Though they may have graduated from high school years or even decades ago, devoted alumni make the trip to Koshien to root for their alma mater. Meanwhile, the rest of the country seems glued to TV sets all day long, following the fates of youngsters destined to be tomorrow's pro stars.

Stars also blossom in college baseball, and since 1925 the Tokyo Six University League has been the flowerbed of college talent. Made up of Waseda, Keio, Meiji, Hosei, Rikkyo, and Tokyo universities, the league is a further link to the roots of the Japanese game.

The Tokyo Six tournament draws fairly big crowds but does not capture the nation's fancy the way the high-school tournament does. This was not always the case. Prior to the flourishing of the pro game, college baseball was the most popular spectator sport in the country. In fact, college baseball actually helped lay the groundwork for the professional game in Japan. In 1905 Waseda University became the first Japanese baseball team to travel to the U.S. Returning to Japan, Waseda helped develop and popularize baseball in its nascent stages, incorporating ideas the players and coaches had learned on the U.S. tour.

College baseball's popularity peaked in the 1920s. Once professional baseball started, the best players began to skip college to join the pro ranks. The history of the game was forever changed with the introduction of professionalism. Even so, the professional ranks owe a debt of gratitude to the high-school and college games for first popularizing baseball in Japan.

2

STRATEGY

A WALK, a sacrifice bunt, and a "timely two-base hit": this is the offensive strategy of Japanese baseball. Pervading all levels of the sport is the belief that the team that scores first usually wins. All the old sayings about how difficult it is to play catch-up ball are hauled out time and again by Japanese managers. While there is some merit to the score-first theory, it makes for an extremely conservative brand of baseball. There are certainly no Whitey Herzog there's-war-on-them-there-base-paths types or Earl Weaver "pitching, defense, and a three-run homer" theorists in the dugouts of Japanese ballparks.

The beauty of baseball is its timelessness. A baseball game is a contest played until someone wins, even if curfew laws interfere and the game has to be continued the following day. Right?

Wrong. In Japan there is an actual time limit on a baseball game, a restriction that results in tie games. In the Pacific League the time limit is four hours or 12 innings. Until 1990 the Central League had a 12-inning rule but has begun an experiment aimed at eliminating ties by extending tie games to 15 innings. Though stadium regulations vary slightly, in general tie games may be continued the following day, unless the teams are scheduled elsewhere that day. Ties will also be allowed to stand when teams have travel commitments, stadiums are booked, or there are no open dates on the schedule.

Tie games actually count in the standings, and at times it does seem that clubs play more not to lose than to win. But since ties account for approximately only 4 percent of all ballgames, much of the controversy over tie games is about a margin so miniscule that it causes mathematical headaches only for statisticians. But the tie policy can lead to bizarre situations like a best-of-seven Japan Series that becomes a best-of-eight series. And occasionally the policy can wreak havoc, as happened during the 1988 Pacific League pennant race. To take the pennant, the Kintetsu Buffaloes needed to win both ends of a season-ending doubleheader with the Lotte Orions. Kintetsu won the first game but time ran out on the second, the game ended in a tie, and the Seibu Lions took the pennant. During the regular season Kintetsu had won more games but Seibu finished .002 percentage points ahead in the final tally.

The main problem with eliminating tie games has to do with the very reason a time limit was established in the first place: noise. As was the case in the controversy over installing lights at Chicago's Wrigley Field, people residing near stadiums in Japan do not want to be bothered by late-night noise and the accompanying traffic congestion. The odd thing is that even afternoon games are affected by the tie rule. Pacific League games that start at 2:30 p.m. still have to be wrapped up by 6:30 p.m.

Another argument for time limits has to do with transportation to and from games. The very West Coast idea of driving to the ballpark hardly exists in Japan's densely populated cities; commuter service is vital to baseball's survival. Proponents of time limits argue that since trains do not run all night, games must end before midnight to allow fans to get home. In response, starting times for some night games have been moved up, allowing most extra-inning contests to finish well before midnight.

The attitude toward tie games is definitely changing, and tie games may eventually disappear. But eliminating ties will not change the play-for-one-run approach to baseball, since one run is all that's needed to break a tie. Thus, the inner game of baseball will continue to thrive in Japan. That game revolves around bunting.

Bunts, if executed with daring and surprise, create excitement on the field. Base runners are off on a tear, fielders charge this way and that, pitchers get rattled, hitters either fake the bunt and slap a single, or drag bunt and try to beat it out for a hit. The key to the strategy is surprise but the Japanese use of the bunt amounts to overkill. The idea of moving the runner to scoring position is entrenched in the Japanese psyche, even when it is not the best move to make.

One thing the rule about tie games will change is the amount of time pitchers waste during extra-inning contests. No longer can pitchers consider 12 innings the be-all and end-all of existence. But to change a pitcher's mindset is extremely difficult, as Japanese pitching strategy follows a route that makes for extremely long games.

Japanese pitchers love to work the count, to nibble the corners trying to give hitters fits. The strategy is sound when the pitcher is ahead in the count and wants the batter to chase a bad ball. But instead of going at hitters with their best pitches and looking for strikeouts, Japanese pitchers waste too many pitches. You can test this idea by noting how often the count goes full during a game. This predictability is something you can rely on when deciding when to race to the concession stand. If the count is 0 and 2 (or perhaps I should say 2 and 0, as scoreboards in Japan count strikes first and balls second), you can be fairly sure that three consecutive balls are coming up. Now is the time to dash off to get your fried squid; you'll be back in time to see the payoff pitch. This drawn-out method of pitching makes for a lot of games that last three hours or more, so be sure to bring a cushion to last the distance.

Dragging the game out even further is a pitcher change and the subsequent mound conference, involving the pitcher, the catcher, the four infielders, the manager, and perhaps an interpreter! On the mound, the pitcher is so paranoid that he talks with his glove over his mouth, supposedly to prevent his instructions from being lip-read by the opposing team.

Pitchers may be culprits but they are also victims of Japanese baseball. To stay warm between innings, most Major League pitchers don a team jacket to keep their arms from stiffening up while they're off the mound. In contrast, Japanese hurlers continue light throwing while their team is at bat. And throwing practice doesn't end on a pitcher's off day. Throwing between starts is almost compulsory, supposedly showing the manager that responsibility isn't being shirked.

With this training regimen, it is not surprising that many Japanese pitchers do not last long. Those who survive are saved by a 130-game schedule, which in theory means fewer starts than Major Leaguers with their 162-game slate. But nowadays Japanese aces aren't hurling as many innings as past pitchers did. Following the Major League trend that began in the 1970s, the era of the bullpen stopper has arrived. These days Japan has its Goose Gossage and Rollie Fingers types to relieve starting pitchers.

In the early days of Japanese baseball, pitching stars were logging 300-plus innings per season, but today the total is down in the low 200s. A young Japanese hurler still throws far more pitches than Major Leaguers, but precious arms are being preserved to lengthen careers, to the obvious benefit of clubs. As these lively young arms are receiving better treatment, pitching is bound to improve.

On the other hand, batters in Japan have a long way to go to catch up to Major League standards. The similarity of batting stances at all levels of Japanese baseball gives intelligent pitchers a distinct advantage over hitters. Japanese players tend to bat in something of a golf stance, feet apart and aligned with the shoulders swinging through the ball on an even plane. Many Japanese batters are excellent slap hitters and good at fouling off pitches to stay in the batter's box. There are also enough home-run hitters to prevent pitchers from becoming complacent and thinking that all batters hit for average. Still, it's rare to see open or closed stances a la Rod Carew, who had different stances for different pitchers. Nor will you see any Rickey Henderson crouch-type stances that narrow the strike zone. Switch hitting too is rare.

Distinct hitting styles simply do not exist in Japanese baseball. Whereas Major League practice is to let a hitter develop a batting stance he is comfortable with, the Japanese player is told which stance to use. Deviations from those instructions do not fit coaches' theories.

The excuse that since Japanese players are smaller they have to learn how to go with the pitch and spray the ball to all fields is just that, an excuse. Weight training can add needed muscle to any hitter, enabling him to add power to his swing. Swinging with a slight uppercut can cause balls to be driven into gaps for doubles and triples. One encouraging development for better batting has been the construction of Major League-size ballparks like Tokyo Dome, which will likely force players to improve their batting skills.

Defensively, many Japanese glovemen are sound, as playing on some of the all-dirt infields requires greater concentration to contain the wild bounces produced by uneven surfaces. In contrast to infield play, outfield play is sorely in arrears. Throwing out runners and holding runners to singles instead of doubles are undervalued skills. Japanese outfielders have notoriously weak arms, something that has increased the importance of the cutoff man. A theory has developed that the Japanese are very good at hitting the cutoff man. There may be some truth to the claim but the cutoff man usually comes so far out into the outfield that by the time he turns to relay the ball to home, it's too late to catch the runner. In their defense, outfielders do seem to play the wall better than Major Leaguers; the unusually high fences and the shorter distances to those fences provide them much more practice playing the wall.

To improve their skills Japanese do practice much more than their Major League counterparts. Also, it is often claimed that Japanese players are in better shape than Major Leaguers. This may have been true in the past, when Major Leaguers treated the six-week spring training as a chance to work off the excess weight gained during the winter, but today's player is expected to be in shape when spring training starts. With vast fortunes enticing them, today's Major Leaguers have the incentive to be in shape. Generally speaking, they are in as good a shape as the Japanese prior to and over the course of the season.

Like Japanese businessmen, Japanese baseball players put in considerable overtime hours. Even when the season is completed, it doesn't really end. There is light autumn training, followed by a league-enforced rest period through the winter, during which players are expected to train on their own. Then comes spring training, which opens on February 1! Yes. Batting, fielding, and pitching practice start in earnest in the throes of winter. Of course, the clubs hightail it for warmer climes in southern Japan (Okinawa or Kyushu) or overseas. The Giants train on the island of Guam, the Chunichi Dragons go to Australia, and Kintetsu visits Saipan. Some Japanese clubs have also held spring training in the U.S.; since 1978 the Yakult Swallows have set up camp in Yuma, Arizona. With the yen strong, the idea makes economic sense. Meanwhile, the state of Arizona is so pleased with the results that in February it hosts the largest annual Japanese business and cultural festival in the U.S., appropriately called Japan Week.

The Giants too have made use of Arizona, sending their young players to the winter instructional league. Sadly, the Major League clubs, led by Oakland A's vice president of operations Sandy Alderson, recently increased the entry fee from $3,500 per team per season to $100,000. The Seibu Lions and the Taiyo Whales had also been planning to send players but the fee hike has curtailed Japanese participation until a better agreement can be worked out. Spring training in Arizona by Japanese clubs has, as yet, not been affected by disagreements over money.

Many Major Leaguers are bemused by the bizarre training the Japanese go through at camp, where everything is so organized that players have no time to think. The overall atmosphere is like that of an army boot camp. Meals are often eaten on the field during breaks. Drill, drill, drill is the common procedure, as endless hours are spent running over hill and dale, stopping only for calisthenics.

The seemingly endless hours of batting, fielding, and pitching practice are meant to perfect skills. Rest is not a word in the Japanese manager's vocabulary. This system is never questioned, as Japanese are not very good at challenging authority. Throughout the season practice continues on off-days and before games.

The problem with practice lies not in the hours put in but in the effective use of time. As the saying goes, practice makes perfect. But unlike the Japanese business community, which has copied good ideas from outside and adapted them for local use, Japanese baseball is gridlocked in the past. Managers are trapped into thinking that there is only one way to win baseball games. The basic theory is that hard work can compensate for lack of talent. Major League managers know that both hard work and talent are needed; they also know there are many different ways to win a ballgame.

Forcing players to play with an injury is a common mistake of Japanese managers, who rarely look beyond the next pitch in forming game strategy. These managers do not understand that a club is composed of 25 individuals and that for maximum results each individual needs to be treated differently. This narrowmindedness is one reason why Japanese are such poor teachers and why there is such a lack of depth in the Japanese baseball system. Japan has a huge population that will continue to produce players but the infrastructure in place does not provide the competitiveness needed for development of professional-level skills.

The Japanese minor leagues are made up of 12 teams that are farm clubs of the professional teams. All clubs retain the parent-team names, and they play out of the same stadium when the parent club is on the road. The Eastern League consists of the farm teams of Seibu, Yomiuri, Nippon Ham, Yakult, Lotte, and Taiyo; in the Western League are Daiei, Hiroshima, Orix, Hanshin, Kintetsu, and Chunichi.

The farm teams generate little public interest and are really nothing more than reserve teams that play each other. Whereas the Major Leagues have rookie, A, AA, AAA, and winter leagues, where competition is keen and instruction valuable, the Japanese minors wallow in mediocrity and obscurity. If Japanese baseball were to market and move minor-league clubs to cities without professional franchises, the minors would likely improve. If young players had the chance to play before crowds, experience game tension, and learn how to win, they would mature into seasoned players much more rapidly. Instead, minor-league games in Japan are played before empty stands, sometimes on less than adequate playing surfaces. Many games are nothing more than glorified scrimmages, completely lacking in intensity.

Another problem with Japanese baseball is that too many players joining pro teams straight from high school are largely out of their depth at too young an age. Granted, there are exceptions, like Seibu's Kazuhiro Kiyohara, who burst on the pro scene and made an immediate impact. A much-vaunted graduate of the prestigious PL Gakuen high-school championship team, Kiyohara hit 31 homers his first year out of high school. But the majority of high-school picks need to be seasoned in the minors. And with only one minor league in Japan, there is no opportunity for a player to work his way up through the system. Instead, all the developmental work has been done in high school.

Because of this limited organization, the Japanese probably miss out on the late bloomer. It is possible for late bloomers to play college ball for four years, then try to make the leap to the professional level. A disadvantage is that college ball in Japan is not as well coached as it is in the U.S. The only other option for players not drafted is to play in the various industrial leagues and hope to get noticed by scouts before they're forced to give up their professional dreams.

Better coaching is probably the biggest key to the future development of Japanese baseball. Unless managers start to break away from traditional thinking and look at what they can learn from the Major Leagues, professional baseball in Japan will continue to lag far behind the American game. But a Japanese manager's life is not an easy one, and taking chances can be dangerous. A manager is often forced by ownership to apologize publicly to fans if the team is doing poorly. It's no wonder Japanese managers tend to hide out in the corner of the dugout all game long.

Foreign coaches and managers have been employed in Japan with some success. The language barrier is always cited as the major stumbling block but baseball has a universal language of its own. The Seibu Lions employed Bert "Campy" Campaneris, the speedy base-stealing shortstop of the mid 1970s champion Oakland A's, as a base-running coach, and the results were very encouraging. Jim Lefebvre, Jim Marshall, Bart Shirley, and others have also coached in Japan.

At the management level, there have been some notable successes. Wally Yonamine, a nisei from Honolulu, spent years as a player and coach before guiding the Chunichi Dragons to a Japan Series title. Being fluent in Japanese greatly contributed to his success. Former Major Leaguer Don Blasingame was not fluent in Japanese but did have playing, coaching, and managing experience in Japan. In 1979 he guided the Hanshin Tigers, Japan's worst professional team when he took over, to the .500 level and respectability. The experience of Blasingame and the others proves that it is possible for foreigners to coach and manage, but it is also true that the insular nature of Japanese baseball is a hard obstacle to overcome.

Japan proved it can compete on a global scale when it took the 1984 Olympic baseball crown in Los Angeles, in the process defeating a strong American side composed of top college stars. But for Japan to compete consistently at the highest level, the talent has to be let loose under a more open system of play. In North America, there is a quantum leap in caliber from college ball to the Major League level. Given that last year's high-school stars often obtain starting positions on Japanese pro teams, it seems safe to say that Japanese pro baseball more resembles AAA-level rather than Major League baseball. In North America a Dwight Gooden-type leap from the low minors to all-star status in the Majors at a tender age is rare. In Japan it's the norm, as top high-school stars are expected to leap on the pro scene with a vengeance.

Although Japanese baseball is bound to improve in the future, it will never reach the Major League level unless attitudes change drastically. To separate sports and culture, however, is difficult in any society. Whether the cultural influence is an asset or a detriment to sporting progress is beside the point; sports and culture are tightly intertwined.

3

FANS

AS YOU ENTER a professional-baseball stadium in Japan, you're struck by the noise. You ask yourself, "What's going on? Have I missed the first inning? Who scored?"

Relax. The fans are just warming up.

Games in Japan attract both home and visiting fans. The most fervent, like those in America, sit in the bleachers. But the bleachers in a Japanese ballpark aren't anything like those in America, where diehard fans mix with beer-swilling sun worshippers in various states of undress. A different kind of party atmosphere exists in Japan.

The home fans are always seated in the right-field bleachers, while the visiting fans take the left-field stands. Before you begin to have visions of rampaging hordes of soccer hooligans about to charge each other, take a look around. There are a lot of families packed into these bleacher sections; these fans are here strictly to cheer on their favorite teams. There is little chance of violence in these bleachers but this is definitely where the action is.

The teams themselves employ cheerleaders (*ōendan,* in Japanese) to lead the cheers. Although they don't form pyramids or spin on their heads a la American college cheerleaders, the *ōendan* can easily match the enthusiasm of their American counterparts. With the help of a band of trumpeters, a few muscular types to wave the enormous team flags, and sometimes troops of pompom girls, the cheer sections are able to fire up the crowd and perhaps their field heroes too.

The cheering is very rhythmic in nature, with specific cheers prepared for each batter. The repetitive nature can be grating, as often the cheering doesn't at all reflect the ebb and flow of the game. The constant noise, pitch after pitch, makes many Japanese hitters masters of concentration, able to block out almost any racket. And to those batters who need the extra boost, the cheering is a source of strength. These cheer sections are intensely loyal, never turning on the team even when it's losing miserably. Through thick and thin, these fans stay fans.

The basic cheer, roughly the equivalent of our we-want-a-hit cry, goes *kattobase* followed by a player's name, e.g., *kattobase Ikeyama.* Variations are done to the Mickey Mouse theme song, the Popeye theme song, or themes from Japanese TV programs like the Ultraman superhero series of the 1960s. Every time a batter makes an out, the opposing fans sarcastically cheer his misfortune. A home run or key hit results in a banzai cheer, yelled with both arms raised, like a football referee signaling a touchdown. The banzai cheer is often accompanied by confetti-throwing and intense waving of the monster team flags, all in all a very impressive display of joy. The North American-style seventh-inning stretch does not exist, but at the start of the seventh inning, called *rakkii sebun* (lucky seven) in Japanese, fans in the bleachers release streams of balloons.

To some degree, spontaneity is lacking among Japanese fans but they do know their baseball. Fans respond to runners taking the extra base, outfielders hitting the cutoff man, the well-executed pitchout to catch a base stealer, the big home run or strikeout. But if you're plopped into the middle of a game, the cheering will reveal only which team is at bat, not who's winning.

At any ballpark silence is a rare commodity, a situation that is both a blessing and a curse. In North America you might be tempted to go to a ballgame just to relax, but you can't do that easily in Japan. On the other hand, you'll never encounter a coma-like atmosphere brought on by lackluster play; Japanese fans will not put up with that. They take their baseball very seriously, and the loud cheering reflects the common belief that every game should be played at Pete Rose intensity.

These enthusiastic fans are Japanese baseball's source of energy. The cheerleaders are decked out in special outfits, from a colorful kimono-style jacket called a *happi* to a T-shirt adorned in team colors with the logo prominently displayed. The giant, swooping team flags lend a splash of carnival atmosphere to the game, and the clarion cries of trumpeters lead the cheering.

The fans themselves rhythmically clap out the cheers with a plastic instrument called a cheer bat or cheer megaphone. Young fans plaster their cheer bats with stickers displaying the names and numbers of their favorite players. Many clubs issue special caps to their junior fan-club members. Children are also given significant discounts on bleacher seats and seats down the left- and right-field lines. A quarter or even a half of the price of an adult ticket, these discount tickets create fan loyalty at an early age. On any weekend or school holiday you'll see the bleachers filled with children.

Fans often have to line up hours before the game to get a seat in these unreserved bleacher sections. For Giants' games fans will sleep overnight on the pavement to assure themselves a good spot in line. But it is not just Giants' games that draw crowds. Good weather, a holiday, or an intriguing matchup can also bring the crowds out.

Due to the distance between cities, visiting fans usually attend games in great numbers only on weekends. Still, many people living in Tokyo were not born there. The capital city attracts people from all over Japan, so any club can attract a good share of support when it visits Tokyo. The Hanshin Tigers have an especially large number of fans who turn out to support Osaka's team on visits to Tokyo. And many school trips include visits to ballparks, hence the appearance of large groups of uniform-clad youngsters in some sections of the stadium.

As team sponsors, the companies themselves encourage employees to turn out and support the company team at the ballpark. The ploy may be a form of corporate blackmail but going to a game beats putting in overtime at the office, and a free ticket is a free ticket in anybody's book. Of course, a free ticket to a Giants' game is a highly coveted item.

Giants' fans, the robotrons of Japanese baseball fandom, show up no matter where the game is held. These fans invariably turn out en masse, always moving about with trooplike organization. Their sheer numbers often lift the spirits of Giants' players. Given the Giants' tradition and history, Yomiuri has to do little advertising to attract fans. This smugness has rubbed off on the fans, who believe in something like the Giants' divine right to victory.

Critics charge that the Giants have too much power but an opposite view holds that the Giants are great for Japanese baseball. To some extent, fan sentiment is polarized along Giants' and anti-Giants' lines. The personification of this anti-Giants' feeling is found in the followers of the Hanshin Tigers, Osaka's pride and joy, and historically the Giants' chief rival.

Since Japanese baseball began, the Giants have steamrollered to championship after championship, while the Tigers have continually fallen short. The Giants-Tigers rivalry parallels the great Yankees-Red Sox rivalry in the American League. It was once said that cheering for the Yankees was akin to cheering for General Motors. The Giants hold this corporate ground in Japan.

In North America, cheering for Boston has long meant being frustrated at the Red Sox' inability to beat the Yankees in close pennant races and the Sox' ultimate failures in postseason play. In Japan, Hanshin has traditionally worn the frustrating underdog label.

But the Tigers' failure on the playing field has little effect on their crazy, fun-loving fans. For one thing, Hanshin will always be supported because it represents Osaka in that city's ongoing battle with Tokyo. Osaka is Japan's second city and Tokyoites tend to look down at Osakans for their gruff, salt-of-the-earth natures. On the other hand, Osaka people consider Tokyoites cultural snobs, always thinking they're the best at everything.

This highly charged rivalry always makes for exciting baseball when the sets of fans converge. The volcano burst in 1985, when Hanshin won the Central League pennant after a 21-year wait. In the weeks toward the end of the regular season, Tigers' fans displayed their loyalty in bizarre ways, like shaving their heads and imprinting victory slogans on their scalps. But certainly the most bizarre tale was of a famous Osaka television celebrity who announced she would marry the first man she saw once the Tigers clinched the pennant. Past history suggested that she was relatively safe in avoiding the walk down the aisle but this time the seemingly impossible happened. The celebrity was eventually forced to do an about-face, announcing that she would "date" the lucky guy she met on the day the Tigers clinched the pennant. Her fanaticism is typical of Tigers' fans, who are insanely in love with their team.

If you can go to just one game in Japan, take in a Tigers-Giants matchup in Nishinomiya (between Osaka and Kobe) for full-bore crowd pandemonium. For many people the highlight isn't really the game itself but the train trip to Koshien Stadium on the Hanshin Line. Hanshin fans adorn themselves in bright Tiger-yellow clothes; they sing and perform Tigers' cheers on the platforms while they wait for trains. In this land of reserved demeanor and controlled response, the joy of Tigers' fans is something to behold.

After the Tigers and Giants, the rest of the teams scramble for whatever support they can obtain. One of the more successful clubs is the Seibu Lions, who have managed to tap the youth and family markets through creative marketing. Lions' fans are not as crazy as Tigers' fans or as fiercely proud as Giants' fans, but Seibu has managed to secure a middle range of supporters, people who like their baseball served up in style.

The other Tokyo clubs are left with extremely localized support. The Nippon Ham Fighters have always been seen as the poor cousins of the Yomiuri Giants, with whom they share Tokyo Dome (and little else!). When Nippon Ham is winning, fans turn out, as winners in Tokyo are supported to the nth degree. But at too many Nippon Ham games empty seats outnumber fans. With the advent of Tokyo Dome and all the curiosity it has brought, Nippon Ham has been able to draw well. But how many of those people are there to see the new stadium and how many are there to root for Nippon Ham? That question won't be answered until the newness of the Dome wears off.

One advantage of attending a Nippon Ham game is that you get the chance to kick back, stretch out among the empty seats, and take a break from the Tokyo chaos. Catch up on the latest political scandal with your neighbor, eat out the concession stand until you explode, or just enjoy the ballgame at your own pace. At Nippon Ham games you create your own atmosphere.

The Yakult Swallows garner up those Tokyoites who like the Central League but not the Giants. Swallows' fans, some of whom are crazy characters indeed, especially love to annoy the opposing pitcher when he gives up a run. When that happens, the entire right-field-bleacher section pops open plastic umbrellas to tell the pitcher it's time he headed for the showers. Swallows' fans rely on their sarcastic sense of humor to get through seasons in which they are often outshouted at home by visiting fans.

The suburban areas (if you can call Kawasaki and Yokohama suburban areas) draw two diametrically opposed sets of fans. The Lotte Orions are saddled in Kawasaki, the heart of the pollution belt of greater Tokyo. The sparse crowd gathered at the ballpark can be seen laughing, talking, fighting, sleeping, doing everything except supporting the Orions. Character, Kawasaki Stadium has it in bucketloads. But any real baseball atmosphere is lost, as Lotte fans seem preoccupied with anything except what is happening on the field.

In contrast, Yokohama is a city bursting with pride. Fiercely loyal and extremely friendly, Yokohama fans deserve better baseball than what the Whales have given them over the years. (The Whales won their only Central League pennant and Japan Series in 1960.) Thanks to those steep banks of seats in Yokohama Stadium, Whales' fans are literally right on top of the action. Unfortunately they seem a bit too nice for the Japanese baseball scene. Maybe it's those sea breezes that cool off the heat of the moment but Whales' fans never seem very interested in giving the opposition fits.

Chunichi supporters routinely coat Nagoya Stadium in Dragon blue. They too are very loyal to their team, requiring only that Chunichi be competitive and pick up an occasional pennant. These fans are among the nicest in the entire country, and completely lack the brashness often seen in fans of the bigger clubs in Tokyo and Osaka.

As mentioned earlier, Hanshin Tigers' fans are among the most spirited in the country. Kansai (the Osaka-Kobe-Kyoto region) has two other teams, the Orix BlueWave and the Kintetsu Buffaloes; both have fanatical supporters but their numbers are never huge. The atmosphere at either home ballpark is not half as rabid as what you find at Koshien any day of the season. Kintetsu's Fujiidera Stadium is located between Osaka and Nara, so Kintetsu draws fans from both cities. Orix picks up the leftovers of Osaka and Kobe who are not Hanshin fans.

Further west are the Hiroshima Carp fans, a very certifiable bunch indeed. The bleacher bums at Hiroshima Civic Stadium hurl vicious but humorous barbs at opposing players, all in the gruff Hiroshima dialect. Up there with

Hanshin fans as bona fide hecklers, Carp fans are able to enjoy a ballgame as well as any group in Japan.

Generally speaking, fans in the western part of Japan are livelier than their Tokyo counterparts. In Fukuoka, on Japan's southwestern island of Kyushu, Daiei Hawks' fans occasionally get volatile, though they too know how to kick back and enjoy a game. Baseball fans in Fukuoka went ten years without a team, though they were treated to an occasional pro game played at Heiwadai Stadium. In any case, these fans lost none of their verve or passion for the game.

Part of the fun of going to a ballgame in Japan is watching the fans. The lifeblood of Japanese professional baseball, the fans make the stadiums come alive every spring, summer, and fall. These fans are all similar in their love and enthusiasm for baseball, but somehow each group of fans manages to express its feelings in its own way.

4

STADIUMS

JAPANESE SOCIETY IS often called homogeneous, and there is also a sameness to much of the inner city. Almost any large city you visit has a tangle of telephone lines overhead, mazelike street patterns, and a wonderful chaos of skyscrapers, railway lines, and noodle shops. It is no surprise that at first glance Japanese baseball stadiums too tend to have a certain sameness.

Almost all the ballparks are 91 meters (298 feet) down the right- and left-field lines and 118 meters (387 feet) to the center-field fence. There are no obtuse-shaped fences, like Boston's Fenway Park with its "green monster" left-field fence towering over the left fielder. The construction of Tokyo Dome though, along Major League dimensions, has forced other clubs to make modifications. Many clubs moved their fences back a little or raised the height of outfield fences. In the past these fences tended to be 30 to 40 feet closer to home plate than fences in North American stadiums. Obviously these short porches cheapen the home-run ball, as long line drives or 300-foot fly balls can carry over the fences for round-trippers.

Adjusting parks' dimensions is giving Japanese pitchers a fairer break. The original reasoning behind smaller parks was that Japanese ballplayers were shorter and smaller than Major Leaguers and hence ballparks should be smaller too. Smaller fields also meant that more seats could be crammed into the limited space that most inner-city ballparks occupy. Expanding any city ballpark is bound to impose on the surrounding area. But the winds of change have begun to emanate from Tokyo, and "Dome-ball" will bring more ballparks with Major League dimensions, Green Stadium Kobe being the first example.

Definitely not Major League quality is the seating in many Japanese stadiums. Outside the bleachers, fans who sit in the lower ten to fifteen rows view the game through a kind of netting or fence that resembles chicken wire. Behind home plate you peer through the netting assured that no foul is going to land on your cranium; unfortunately the netting extends down the lines to protect spectators from line drives but at the same time slightly obstructs the view. Granted, there are few poles to block views but the fencing produces a claustrophobic atmosphere in many stadiums. Finally, the medium- to massive-size foul territory at almost every ballpark leaves fans a bit removed from play.

Another problem in stadiums is the pervasive green. No matter what the home team's color scheme is, it is green that is seen almost everywhere in a Japanese ballpark. Fences are green, bullpens are green, the dugouts, the scoreboards, everything nailed down is painted green. Yokohama Stadium, with its blue fences, is a rare exception; elsewhere, things are green-green-green, *until* they're plastered over with advertising.

Most fences ringing the playing field have advertising that consists of bright white lettering on the evergreen backdrop. This dull testimony to commercial crassness is reminiscent of American ballparks in the 1940s, when local and national advertisers competed for space. In Japan the Letraset lettering is uniformly dull, broken only by huge, colorful billboards that tower above some bleachers. Even light poles have not escaped advertising, as neon lettering shines down from the poles that ring Kawasaki Stadium. (There are a few sacred places in ballparks; the dugouts are purified in Shintoist tradition with a mound of salt on dugout steps.)

Lit up on the scoreboard in a traffic-light pattern is the ball and strike count, as mentioned previously, written opposite that of Major League scoreboards, with strikes listed before balls. Of course, S refers to strikes, B to balls, and O to outs. Also on continual display are batting and pitching statistics, updated as the game is played. Here uniformity ends, as each stadium has its own character.

Unique is the best word to describe Tokyo Dome. Japan's first domed stadium is viewed much the way the Houston Astrodome was when it opened in 1965. As that "Eighth Wonder of the World" generated considerable excitement in the U.S. almost 30 years ago, "Dome fever" has now hit Japan. Tours of the Dome are available when there's no ballgame scheduled. How long the novelty will last is anybody's guess.

The Giants and Fighters share this ballpark (as they did the old Korakuen Stadium), and the Fighters have certainly benefited from the new park. Of course, the Giants could play anywhere and sell out every game; but in 1988, their first year in the Dome, the Fighters, a mediocre team at best, averaged a whopping 37,800 fans per game, leading the Pacific League in attendance. But besides the lure of baseball, what else is the attraction of Japan's first domed stadium?

From the outside the inflatable airbag roof looks like a large egg, a shape that has given rise to the Dome's nickname, Big Egg. (Big Egg is also an acronym for the catchphrase Big Entertainment & Golden Games.) Approaching the ballpark from Korakuen Station on the Marunouchi Line or JR's Suidobashi Station, you see the huge egg shape dominating the skyline. The glass awnings and tiled walkways lend an air of modern elegance to the area that used to house rundown Korakuen Stadium. Today the beautiful white cushion atop the aqua concrete shell is a sea of tranquillity amidst the insanity of ugly, overcrowded, downtown Tokyo.

But once you're inside the Dome, you realize that baseball here is too sanitized. The myriad of blue seats gives the place a shopping-mall dullness. Concession stands, garbage cans, restrooms, and stairways are all coordinated, adding to the overall uniformity. The place is great when it's raining outside and you're dying to watch a game. But part of baseball is the sun, the wind, and the temperature, and when the weather's fine, the Dome is not where you want to be. This hermetically sealed structure is simply not the best place to watch baseball. Even the bullpens are sealed and concealed from public view, lying under the stands behind home plate.

When Big Egg is packed, Metrodome levels of noise can be achieved; when it's not full, the sound of the crowd or the voices of high-pitched female announcers tend to echo around the big cavern. Worst of all, the Dome does not look like a ballpark; rather, it resembles a giant

▲ Manager Motoshi Fujita receives a victory toss as the Giants clinch yet another pennant.

▲ The chase is on! After getting hit by a pitch, a Yakult player wants revenge but the Hanshin pitcher heads for the outfield.

▼ And for those who stand and fight . . . Seibu's
Kazuhiro Kiyohara applies a flying body block
to an offending Lotte pitcher.

▲ A Kintetsu fielder somehow manages to hold on to the ball in this spectacular catch.

▲ Enormous team flags are a standard part of a cheer group's equipment.

◄ During a pitcher change the manager is joined by the entire infield for a mound conference.

▲ Fans enjoy the picnic atmosphere of the grass
bleachers.

► A cheerleader tries to get the fans involved by
climbing the fencing that separates spectators
from players and errant line drives.

▲ No, it's not raining. Yakult Swallows' fans open
   their umbrellas to tell the opposing pitcher it's
   time he hit the showers.

carpeted showroom, which is exactly what it becomes when a boat show or car show is in town. Constructing a multipurpose facility may be economically sound but aesthetically it makes no sense.

Being a dome, Big Egg automatically has one strike against it, but at least the seating was designed for baseball, with all seats facing toward home plate. Sightlines are great, so buy a cheap seat, enjoy the game, and spend your yen elsewhere. Even when you're in line for refreshments, you won't miss a pitch, since closed-circuit TVs beam the action into the concourse areas.

And there is a lot more to do here than watch baseball. On the concourse level (with access from outside) you can check out the T-shirts, caps, etc., at Japan's best baseball-souvenir shop. And be sure to go to the Japanese Baseball Hall of Fame & Museum next door. Or admire the architecture from outside and place a bet at the off-track betting facility next to the Dome. Or ride the roller coaster at the amusement park opposite the stadium. You can do it all at Domeland!

Domes may be the current trend in baseball architecture but fans of the outdoor game need not despair; amid the hustle and bustle of Tokyo, Meiji Jingu Stadium, home of the Yakult Swallows, is a treasure. Besides the baseball stadium, the huge sports complex includes rugby and soccer stadiums, and nearby are tennis courts and other recreational facilities. It all adds up to an attractive and spacious sports oasis right in the center of Tokyo.

Fresh-faced school kids lining up for autographs outside the players' entrances, gravelly voiced scalpers hawking tickets, and a friendly staff directing you to the right gate—such features combine to make Jingu a great baseball experience even before you enter the park. Inside, Jingu has a very open feel to it, despite its large capacity (48,785). One reason for the open feeling is that seating is very close to the action on the field. Built in 1926, Jingu is Tokyo's oldest ballpark, but it was renovated in the 1980s and retains an appealing freshness in this age of monstrous modern stadiums.

Leaving Tokyo proper, you can hop a train for Tokorozawa, in Saitama prefecture, and enter Seibu country. Seibu Lions Stadium, home of the Pacific League's powerhouse of recent years, is located in a beautiful spot reminiscent of Dodger Stadium. Seibu built this beauty on what used to be a swamp, Tokorozawa literally meaning swampland. Seibu trains leaving from Ikebukuro and Shinjuku whisk you directly from central Tokyo to the spacious concourse that leads up to the stadium.

In this picturesque country setting the air is pleasant, and you can stretch out on the grass in the bleachers. Yes, the bleachers at Seibu Lions Stadium are grass! Lay out your picnic blanket and enjoy the ballgame. This tidy bank of beautiful green grass is an idyllic setting for watching a game, especially on weekdays when crowds aren't packed in. Occasionally the grass bleachers are roped off for "repairs," so it's wise to check if the bleachers are open the day you want to visit. If you're lucky enough to get a box seat, you can reach it via a special passageway reserved for box-seat holders. There is a small table for the four seats in the box, so lay out the tablecloth and enjoy baseball in class!

Unlike at other stadiums, the huge cheering sections at Seibu Lions Stadium are located down the left- and right-field lines. The bleachers are left for those wanting to commune with nature, and the whole ballpark is surrounded by trees and hills for miles—all of this only 40 minutes from Tokyo! In addition, there are tennis courts, a ski ground, a golf course, a water slide, and an amusement park nearby. If it's an escape from the turmoil of Tokyo and a nice day outdoors that you crave, Seibu Lions Stadium is the place to go.

A marked contrast is Kawasaki Stadium, home of the Lotte Orions, and until recently the tackiest professional ballpark in Japan. Renovation has remedied the stadium's worst problems but the park is hemmed in on all sides and centered smack dab in the middle of one of Japan's most heavily polluted areas. Kawasaki Stadium's days may be numbered though, as it is rumored that the Orions are moving to Chiba prefecture's new Marine Stadium, close to Tokyo Disneyland and the Makuhari Messe international exhibition center.

Numbered days is not a problem Yokohama Stadium should have to face very soon. The Taiyo Whales moved to their new home in 1978, and it remains the best move the club ever made. Yokohama has a rich baseball history, having hosted Japan's first professional night game in 1948 in the old "Gehrig Stadium," the present Yokohama Stadium. You can still see the Lou Gehrig plaque in the right-field bleachers; the Babe Ruth plaque is in left.

Yokohama Stadium is a multipurpose arena that hosts everything from concerts to American-football games. But calling Yokohama Stadium multipurpose does not mean it resembles those concrete-bowl football stadiums of North America. The seats here are steeped at such an angle that you feel right on top of the action. The only serious distraction in the place is the annoying music spewed forth by the organist, often at the most inappropriate time of the game. Walled in a glass booth in the center-field bleachers, "the girl in the glass booth" should have closed on opening night. Even so, on a summer night with the cool breeze blowing off Yokohama Bay, there's no better place to watch baseball. And after the game you can head off on one of those spacious Yokohama avenues, take a walk along the waterfront in Miyashita Park, or hurry over to Chinatown for the best Chinese food in Japan.

Tokyo and its environs' stadiums may be the most sophisticated in the country, but Kansai reveals Japanese baseball's heart and soul. With the exception of Green Stadium Kobe, Kansai ballparks do not reflect modern advances in architecture, but there's no better baseball atmosphere in all of Japan. And all stories about Kansai baseball begin and end at Hanshin Koshien Stadium.

Built in 1924, Koshien is Japan's oldest professional stadium still in use. Without a doubt, this ballpark has it all—tradition, excitement, thrills, chills, and spills. Scene of that national obsession, the high-school baseball tournament, Koshien is also the home of Kansai's favorite sons, the Hanshin Tigers.

Koshien is massive, with an iron framework and girders that are truly imposing. One section of the stands is so steep that it is called the Alps. In summer the place is an oven; ice is sold or handed out to cool off potential sunstroke victims. In short, Koshien is a monument to a simpler era of baseball—no modern glass facades, no controlled temperatures, no luxury boxes, no dome. Instead, the place exudes pure baseball. You can see the pitchers warm up in bullpens located behind see-through outfield fences. Those same fences make for some spectacular wall-climbing catches. At Koshien anything can happen, and some days all of it seems to happen.

If you go north a way, you run into Nishinomiya Stadium, the exact opposite of Koshien and one of Japan's most depressing ballparks. The bad vibes are not due to the field, the stands, the fans, or the ballclub; instead, it's the scoreboard! Its obtrusive size and dark colors cast a shadow over the entire ballpark. Combine the scoreboard with the high back wall behind the bleachers and you have a setting fit for a Nuremburg rally. I used to half expect crowds of swarming Brownshirts to fill the place and hail Orix onward to victory!

By moving to Kobe, Orix has managed to escape this phantom scoreboard. Also with the move, the Braves became the BlueWave, but in the process acquired a new horror for the Orix closet—the new team mascot.

Mascots are not really an important part of Japanese baseball. Almost invisible, the typical mascot is just a cute distraction. The new Orix mascot may be cute; unfortunately it continues the team's history of awful mascots.

The BlueWave used to be the Braves, a name that should have summoned forth an Indian or at least a samurai warrior as team mascot. But the Braves' mascot was some sort of tropical-colored ostrich. Perhaps living in the shadow of Koshien left management groping for ideas to lure folks to the lesser ballpark. In any case, the poor selection of mascots has continued with Orix' latest offering, a baby Neptune called Neppie, who is terminally cute in a cartoonish way. About the only good thing to say about Neppie is that he links Kobe's marine heritage to the ballclub and to the BlueWave name.

Green Stadium Kobe, which is near the waterfront, has a capacity of 35,000, smaller than Nishinomiya's. Smaller does mean better though, as seats are roomier and more comfortable. On the fourth floor of the stadium is the Sky Restaurant, a room with a real view. From the Sky Restaurant, fans can look out over the field and watch the game while they eat. The move to Kobe suggests a step up in class for Orix. It also gives the team a chance to create its own legacy away from the past of the Braves and Nishinomiya Stadium.

The Kintetsu Buffaloes are truly burdened in their search for an identity; they can't even decide where to play. Normally they play their home games at Fujiidera Stadium, which lies between Osaka and Nara, Japan's capital from 710 to 784. This quaint park features colonial white columns that ring the stadium, creating a pleasant and elegant old-world facade. It's almost as if the British Raj had left India and set up shop in Osaka. But the palatialness is lost once you go inside the park. Fujiidera does have a dirt infield but the outfield is yet another blanket of artificial turf.

The bullpens are definitely the park's best feature. Fans in Japan normally have little access to bullpens, many of which are surrounded by high walls or buried under the stands or base lines. But at Fujiidera the bullpen is within easy view; fans can lean in and watch the pen come to life.

The most bizarre feature of Fujiidera Stadium is the giant, clear baseball bubble that serves as a ticket booth outside the entrance to the ballpark. The thing looks ready to grow legs and walk around the neighborhood, like some sort of B-grade movie monster. Inside, cutesy cheerleaders and a tacky organ pumping out inane synth patterns distract from the baseball atmosphere.

These problems could be eliminated though, the overall atmosphere improved, and the Buffaloes could likely develop a real following, as Fujiidera Stadium is located in a pleasant country neighborhood minutes from downtown Osaka. The problem is that Kintetsu won't stay put.

Besides Fujiidera, the Buffaloes play "home" games at Osaka's Nissei Stadium, which is falling apart; at Osaka Stadium, now that the Nankai Hawks have flown the coop for Fukuoka; and worst of all at Nagoya, a good hour by bullet train (*shinkansen*) and a city that already has a professional baseball team. In short, Kintetsu is a team lost in the mysterious "Kansai triangle."

The Daiei Hawks made a wise move in leaving Osaka for Fukuoka and Heiwadai Stadium. This ballpark used to be home to the Lions, until 1978 when Seibu bought the Pacific League club and brought it to the Tokyo area, leaving Fukuoka without a professional team. But the tidy little ballpark did not die, since every year the Seibu Lions would return for a few "home" games, and other teams too occasionally played in Fukuoka.

Heiwadai Stadium is a pretty little park, and beyond the bleachers are trees, hills, and blue skies. As in all Japanese ballparks, there's too much foul territory, and box seats lie quite a way behind home plate. Still, night games at Heiwadai are among the best in Japan. Fukuoka is on the southern island of Kyushu, and nights can be very hot, almost tropical. There is no better way to pass a hot summer night than by watching the Hawks battle one of their Pacific League foes.

The idyllic setting won't last much longer though, as plans are afoot for a domed stadium that will include a hotel, shops, restaurants, and recreation facilities. Modeled on Toronto's Skydome and scheduled to be part of the Fukuoka Twin Dome City project, the glass-encased, air-conditioned ballpark will be another example of Japan's modern baseball architecture. But modernity does not necessarily mean style. While you still can, see a game at Heiwadai; the hollow, shiny shell is not supposed to land in Fukuoka until 1994.

Shiny is exactly the word for the Hiroshima Carp's renovated Civic Stadium. The park now has a second deck running from foul pole to foul pole, increasing capacity to 32,920. This great little stadium is located off a streetcar line right downtown, opposite famous Heiwa

Koen, Peace Park. But somehow the stadium doesn't seem crammed in like other metropolitan parks, even though the bus station towers above it and Genbaku Domu, the Atomic Bomb Memorial, is visible behind the third-base section.

The outfield grass always looks worn but sightlines are tremendous and there are virtually no posts in the small park. The spacious bleachers get plenty of sun, and Hiroshima's climate is conducive to enjoyable baseball. Though summer temperatures can be very hot, the rainy season does not seem to last forever (as it does elsewhere in Japan) and rainouts are rare. All in all, Hiroshima Civic Stadium is Japan's best-kept ballpark secret.

With its flat, gridlike city plan, a legacy from the American Occupation after World War II, Nagoya has been labeled dull by most comers. In contrast, the baseball here is not at all dull, and Nagoya Stadium is yet another treasure among Japanese ballparks. Like Hiroshima's tiny park, Nagoya Stadium has a grass field and seats that are right on top of the action. Though somewhat bland in layout and color scheme, the stadium is a very pleasant place to watch a game, an odd contrast to the factory-dominated environs that surround it. To find the ballpark, head toward the water tower painted with a giant baseball, located just behind the stadium.

Outside the big cities, Japan's countryside cities host games that are a genuine treat to attend. All of the pro clubs play a limited number of "home" games in this hinterland, from Sapporo in the north to Kagoshima in the south. Even if you live in the most isolated place in Japan, chances are once or twice a year a series will be headed your way. These smaller cities and towns have the coziest ballparks in all of Japan, their postage-stamp size making for close contact between fans and players. Of course, many of these parks have extremely short distances to the fences, and home runs fly into nearby residential areas at an incredible rate. If you happen to be in Morioka or Kushiro or one of the other smaller cities where games are played, by all means go. To see a sleepy country town awake to the visit of the stars is an experience not to be missed.

From countryside parks to inner-city stadiums, every Japanese ballpark has its own character, to be sampled and savored with every visit. Baseball is baseball anywhere it's played, but the park it's played in can give the game its own special flavor.

5

RECORDS

868 HOME RUNS, 1,065 stolen bases, 2,215 consecutive games played, 4,490 strikeouts—these are "world" records held by four of Japanese baseball's biggest stars. Sadaharu Oh's 868 home runs beat out Hank Aaron's 755 circuit clouts. Yutaka Fukumoto's 1,065 thefts slide in ahead of Lou Brock's 938 steals. Sachio Kinugasa's 2,215-game streak outlasts the immortal Lou Gehrig's 2,130 consecutive games. And until 1989 Masaichi Kaneda's 4,490 whiffs outgunned Walter Johnson's 3,508 K's. (With over 5,000 strikeouts Nolan Ryan has since blown by both players.)

To many Japanese fans, there is no question about the authenticity of these "world" records, and no mention is made of any difference in caliber between Japanese and Major League ball. Of course, many Major League fans will have none of this. They note that until 1990 the Japanese all-star team had never taken a series from a visiting Major League squad. They also point out that although the Japanese all-stars are genuine stars, the Major League "all-star" squad always includes a number of lesser talented players.

The argument about the relative merits of Japanese and Major League ball will not be settled here. Suffice it to say, Oh, Fukumoto, Kinugasa, and Kaneda were all great baseball players. Given the chance to play in the Majors, all four would have been stars, though whether they would have set the marks they did is debatable. The important point is that Oh hit more home runs and Kinugasa played more consecutive games than any other players in professional baseball, and in these pages their accomplishments are treated as world records.

These achievements are a source of immense pride to Japanese fans. On display at the Japanese Baseball Hall of Fame & Museum at Tokyo Dome are four glass cases containing the uniforms, bats, balls, shoes, and gloves used by Oh, Fukumoto, Kinugasa, and Kaneda. Prominently listed on each display is the date the Japanese player broke the Major League record. For those wishing to witness the historic moments, video histories of Japanese baseball regularly include footage of the games that saw the new records set.

Critics of the world records held by Japanese claim that the players who set them enjoyed unfair advantages. Certainly Oh benefited from the much shorter distances to the fences, in those days 30 to 40 feet closer to home plate than in North American stadiums. If Hank Aaron had batted in Japan's smaller ballparks, his home-run total would have been greater. Oh also faced pitching that was generally weaker than that faced by Aaron.

On the other hand, Aaron had a few advantages. He

broke Babe Ruth's home-run record in his home ball-park, Atlanta-Fulton County Stadium, nicknamed the Launching Pad because of all the home runs hit there. (Of Major League ballparks Atlanta-Fulton County Stadium is the highest above sea level, a height that some people claim allows the ball to carry extremely well in the "rarefied" atmosphere.) After the Braves moved from Milwaukee to Atlanta, Aaron played on a number of mediocre teams. Without the pressure of pennant races, Aaron and his teammates did not face the intense opposition that Oh faced every game in his career.

Oh played for Yomiuri during the golden era that saw the Giants take nine straight Central League pennants and Japan Series championships. Desperate to defeat the Giants anytime they could, the other Central League teams geared up their play when Oh and the Giants came to town. Whereas Aaron stretched out his career as a designated hitter with the Milwaukee Brewers when he was no longer effective as a regular player, Oh retired in top form, clouting 30 home runs his final season. He could have increased his home-run total by extending his career as a DH in the Pacific League but pride and loyalty to the Giants ran deep. After retiring as a player, Oh coached and then managed the Giants.

Statistically Oh comes across the better player, averaging 39.5 home runs over 22 seasons, to Aaron's 32.8 homers over 23 seasons. Oh played the shorter 130-game schedule, compared to Aaron's 162 games, so he had fewer at bats per season to accomplish his feat. Oh not only managed to set the all-time home-run record playing fewer games and fewer seasons, he surpassed Aaron's record by a hefty margin, more than 100 home runs. Oh won a total of 15 home-run titles, including a remarkable 13 in a row; Aaron won four home-run titles.

Anyone who has seen Oh hit is impressed. He batted Mel Ott style, assuming a flamingo batting stance and typically slicing the ball into the stands with his samurai-sword swing. As he revealed in his autobiography, Oh perfected his skills with discipline and training that included elements of Zen meditation and traditional swordsmanship. Part Chinese, he suffered as a youth, growing up in a society intolerant of persons of mixed ancestry. Still, he rose above the problem and became a true professional in every respect. His world record is certainly the equivalent of Aaron's numbers, even given differences between Japanese and Major League ball.

Another record hard to dispute is Sachio Kinugasa's streak of 2,215 consecutive games. The debate over Japanese vs. Major League ball is simply irrelevant to this record. Kinugasa's streak is a reflection of his durability, the ability to play through injury and adversity, and the talent to hold a starting position over the years.

His American counterpart, Yankee great Lou Gehrig, suffered through tremendous physical adversity, contracting amyotrophic lateral sclerosis, a neuromuscular disease now commonly called Lou Gehrig's disease, during his long playing streak. On May 2, 1939, Gehrig finally pulled himself out of the lineup, putting an end to both the 14-season playing streak and all the talk about it in the daily press.

Though he did not suffer a life-threatening disease, Kinugasa had a difficult early life. Born of a Japanese mother and an American G.I. father who left his mother at an early age, Kinugasa suffered the prejudices and hardships commonly faced by Amerasian children left behind after the Occupation. His courage in overcoming those prejudices stood him in good stead in his baseball career, obviously contributing to his ability to play through injury and stay in the lineup. As he approached Gehrig's record, there were certainly times when Kinugasa was playing just to keep the streak alive; still, he was in the lineup for every game during his final season.

Gehrig and Kinugasa share another characteristic; both played in the shadows of other baseball greats, Gehrig behind Babe Ruth and Kinugasa behind Koji Yamamoto, a feared slugger of the 1970s who clouted 536 home runs during his career.

The 1970s also produced the world's greatest base stealer, Yutaka Fukumoto. Sadly, Fukumoto's effect on Japanese baseball has been miniscule, as the stolen base has never been fully utilized in Japan.

In the Major Leagues, Lou Brock and Maury Wills elevated the steal to the offensive-weapon status it holds today. Top Major League base runners consistently rack up nearly 100 steals per season. Teams like the St. Louis Cardinals have raised the steal to an art form, actually winning championships with their speed, even when they lacked home-run power.

Due to managers' conservative strategies and a lack of base-stealing talent, Japan has yet to produce a team feared for its speed. In that light, Fukumoto's accomplishments are all the more remarkable. In 1972 he stole 106 bases during a 130-game schedule; adjusted for the longer Major League season, that figure comes out to a whopping 132 steals. Fukumoto is so far ahead of his base-stealing colleagues that his record is sure to stand for decades.

Brock's record of 938 stolen bases was set over 19 seasons of Major League play, but Fukumoto broke that record after 16 seasons. Also, Fukumoto averaged more steals per season than Brock, 53.9 to 49.4. In Brock's defense, he faced better pickoff moves from opposing pitchers and the stronger throwing arms of Major League catchers. Japanese pitchers are notoriously poor at keeping runners close to base, and catchers don't possess the rifle arms of players like Johnny Bench.

Even in Japan Fukumoto is rarely mentioned in the same breath with the other greats, for one reason because he played his entire career in the Pacific League, which is generally considered inferior to the Central League. This neglect is unfair to Fukumoto, since his team, the Hankyu Braves, won seven pennants and three straight Japan Series championships during his career. Upon breaking Brock's theft record, Fukumoto did receive a special gold-plated base (on display at the Japanese Baseball Hall of Fame & Museum) but he remains Japan's most unknown star. Other stars have maintained high profiles after retirement, but Fukumoto has worked quietly as a coach and manager for Hankyu and Orix.

Unlike Major League greats Lou Brock and Rickey Henderson, both of whom possessed qualities of Olympic-time sprinters, Fukumoto was not imposing physically. His story proves that physical qualities alone do not account for base-stealing success. A low center of gravity, anticipation, knowledge about opposing pitchers, basic baseball sense, and above-average speed combined to make Fukumoto a base-stealing star. His world record too is certainly valid, though even in Japan it is not considered as spectacular as Oh's, in part due to the greater "star" appeal a home-run hitter normally has over a speedster.

Whether or not Masaichi Kaneda's 4,490 strikeouts are a world record is no longer worth debate, as Nolan Ryan has blazed off into the ozone with well over 5,000 strikeouts. But Kaneda did hold the record for a time, after he passed the old Washington Senators' Walter Johnson and his 3,508 K's.

As was common in Japanese baseball in the 1950s and '60s, Kaneda was both a starting pitcher and a relief pitcher, altogether appearing in approximately 35 percent of his team's games. (That's like Roger Clemens starting 35 games a season and relieving in 20 more!) In 1958 Kaneda pitched 332.3 innings, won 31 games, and struck out 311 batters! Suffering arm stress, he stood up to this abuse and demanded proper rest between starts. He realized that the insane schedule would shorten his career and in 1964 declared himself a free agent and jumped to the Giants. There he began to train on his own and rejected the common throw-until-you-drop mentality, earning himself the name "Emperor" Kaneda. The royal title bespeaks both his greatness and his fiery independence, often attributed to the fact that he was born in Japan of Korean parents. Kaneda's record has faded under Nolan Ryan's fastball but Kaneda himself refuses to disappear. He has served as manager of the Orions and led them to their only Japan Series title in 1974.

Oh, Kinugasa, Fukumoto, and Kaneda are Japanese baseball's prime record holders, worthy athletes who could have been stars anywhere. As mentioned previously, the debate about Japanese baseball vs. Major League baseball will be left to others. But until all Japanese ballparks conform to Major League dimensions and the general caliber of Japanese baseball improves, "world" records set by Japanese stars will be suspect.

Still, records are not everything, and Japan's greatest baseball player is not known for his records. That player is Shigeo Nagashima, also known as Mr. Giants, the most beloved baseball player in Japan. Even today Nagashima's face turns up in countless commercials, and his voice can be heard commenting on everything from the Super Bowl to the French presidential election.

To some extent, Nagashima's reputation is based on the way he carried himself as a star during the years the Yomiuri Giants won their record nine consecutive championships. In essence, he was what the Japanese wanted in a star. He had class and education, and dedicated himself to perfecting his skills. Conforming to the ideal of Japanese behavior, Nagashima was humble, respected his coaches, and trained harder than anyone else on the team.

The training paid off, as Nagashima became a powerful slugger (444 home runs) and a superb third baseman. He was the team leader when it counted, as evidenced by his four Japan Series MVP awards. Perhaps more than anything else, Nagashima had a flair for the dramatic. In particular, two events helped put his name at the very top of the list of Japan's superstars.

In May 1959 the Emperor and Empress of Japan attended a Giants-Tigers game at Tokyo's Korakuen Stadium, adding a rare royal touch to this always spirited rivalry. As if planned specifically for the renowned visitors, Nagashima came up to bat in the bottom of the ninth with a chance to win the ballgame. One home run later an unforgettable chapter of the Nagashima legend was set in stone.

The event that capped the legend was Nagashima's tearful farewell speech in 1974. His address to fans who had worshipped his every move came straight from the heart and is forever etched in the collective memory of Japanese baseball fans. With the humility of a Lou Gehrig, the popularity of a Babe Ruth, and the clutch play of a Joe DiMaggio, Shigeo Nagashima was an immortal among mortals. Japanese baseball today yearns for a player whose play can grip the entire nation the way Naga-shima's did.

Future heroes and possible record breakers may be among us now. Baby-faced fireballer Hideo Nomo of Kintetsu could be another Kaneda in the making. His blazing fastball and twist-and-twirl, back-to-the-batter windup yield strikeout after strikeout. The Giants' brilliant Masaki Saito, he of the microscopic ERA, seems determined to win 20 games every season and could be headed for the Japanese Hall of Fame. Seibu's Hisanobu Watanabe is largely overlooked by the media but pitches his club to pennant after pennant. Gangly Yukihiro Nishizaki of Nippon Ham is shy off the field but one of the fiercest competitors on it. With a smile that breaks fans' hearts and pitches that mow batters down, he delivers a brand of ball that is both fun and fancy. These four young arms may eventually come to hold some of Japanese baseball's pitching records.

On the batting side, Seibu sluggers Kazuhiro Kiyohara or consistent 30 + HR- and 100 + RBI-man Koji Akiyama (who celebrates special home runs with a backflip onto home plate) may creep toward Oh's seemingly unattainable home-run totals. Takahiro Ikeyama, Yakult's hard-hitting shortstop, may be another player to homer his way into history. For his blasts against the center-field screen, Ikeyama has earned the moniker Mr. Backscreen.

One of Japan's best hitters and the country's only three-time Triple Crown winner, Chunichi's Hiromitsu Ochiai continues to pound the hide off the ball, but Ochiai is an unloved oddity in Japan. His foregoing of the regimented training schedule and insistence upon doing things at his own relaxed pace do not endear him to the baseball establishment. While a member of the Lotte Orions he demanded to be traded, eventually landing a very lucrative contract with the Dragons. The tactic got Ochiai what he wanted but smacked of Major-League money-grubbing to the fans. In part due to the weak players' union, most Japanese ballplayers remain loyal to their clubs, accepting management's contract offers without much fuss. Ochiai is tolerated because he delivers the goods but he'll never be the icon Nagashima was. In Ochiai's defense, it's doubtful that any player will be able to live up to Nagashima's exemplary standards.

On the other hand, some player is bound to best the numbers posted by Japanese baseball's world record holders; after all, records are made to be broken. One has only to remember that Babe Ruth's career home-run mark was once thought unattainable; then along came Hank Aaron. It took 40 years after Ruth retired for his record to fall but fall it did.

Regardless of the debate about the credibility of these "world" records, they remain Japanese all-time records. And from the current or future crop of Japanese stars will eventually emerge someone to challenge these records. When that day comes, maybe the caliber of Japanese baseball will no longer be a subject of debate, and a "world" record set in Japan will not have to take a back seat to one set in the West.

6

GAIJIN

THE FOREIGN PLAYER (*gaijin senshu*) is Japanese baseball's necessary evil. Foreign players provide some of the most exciting moments in the game but there are Japanese players and fans who wish the foreigners did not exist. "They can't live with 'em, and they can't live without 'em" perhaps best sums up that attitude. In any case, the predicament of the foreign player is one of the most fascinating aspects of Japanese baseball.

Each team is currently allowed three foreign players, though at any one time only two can be on the parent club. (The unlucky third player waits in the wings as a member of the farm club until he's called up to the parent team.) This restriction is a significant difference from the Major League teams' freedom to sign any player they want, regardless of nationality, and any number of foreign players. The result in the Majors is that though Americans make up the majority of players, there are also significant numbers of Cubans, Mexicans, Venezuelans, etc., playing pro ball in North America.

There is a lot of talk (usually by foreigners) about opening up the Japanese professional game to more foreign players. Such talk is pointless because the Japanese would never allow themselves to become a minority in their own leagues, and that is what could happen if a team could sign any number of foreign players. Foreigners would quickly fill up the rosters of most teams, and their numbers would be self-perpetuating. The presence of so many foreigners on the team would deprive young Japanese players of their only chance to develop skills at the professional level.

The limit on foreign players is not restricted to Japan. European and South American countries set limits on foreign players in their soccer, basketball, and rugby leagues. The Italian professional soccer league, generally thought to be Europe's best, allows three foreign players per club.

Another factor affecting foreign participation in Japanese baseball is money. Japan can't really compete with the United States and Canada, as salaries in Japan are far below those in the Major Leagues, where even utility infielders are millionaires. Japan is left trying to lure either fringe Major Leaguers or declining stars enticed by the prospect of an unusual experience and the substantial monetary gain. Although salaries in Japan are far below those in the Major Leagues, Japanese clubs do pay foreigners far more than what they'd make in AAA ball.

Most of the foreign players are from the United States. Latin players have played in Japan but most of them too have arrived via the minor and Major Leagues of North America. A smaller but still significant group of foreigners is from Taiwan. Long known for its championship

Little League teams, Taiwan did not have a professional outlet for these talented youngsters until 1990. Until that time Taiwanese stars like Genji Kaku, the relief ace of the Chunichi Dragons, had little choice but to try to fulfill their professional dreams in Japan.

Koreans born and raised in Japan play in the Japanese leagues but few Koreans born in Korea choose to play ball in Japan. For one thing, South Korea has its own professional league, made up of seven teams. A 1983 agreement signed by the two countries' baseball associations grants players a certain amount of freedom to play in either country's leagues. Players can move to either country without complicated trades or huge financial deals, but Koreans are still part of the three-*gaijin* quota system in Japan. A greater obstacle is that there is too much prejudice against Koreans to attract large numbers to Japan. No Korean player will tolerate such prejudice when he can be a star in his homeland.

The funniest initial part of a foreign player's life here can easily be the new name he is given. As foreign names are often difficult to pronounce, the Japanese sometimes resort to nicknames. Ask a Japanese about Orix star Greg Wells and he'll have no idea who you are talking about. But mention "Boomer" and he'll likely recognize the name of the first *gaijin* ever to win the Triple Crown here. The name on Wells' uniform is Boomer, and that is also how he is written up in box scores.

If a foreign player's last name is a tongue twister, like that of Gary Rajsich, the Japanese may put the player's first name on his uniform. For this reason, Rajsich became known to the public as Gary (though the Japanese pronunciation is actually something more like Gaarii.) But a few years earlier the name on his brother Dave's uniform was Rajsich!

The brothers Lee, Leron and Leon, posed a different problem. In 1977 when he first came to Japan, Leron Lee was known as Lee. A year later his brother joined him on the Lotte Orions but it would never do to have two Lees on one team. Rather than follow Major League protocol and spell out the brothers' full names in the box scores, the Japanese baseball establishment called Leon Lee simply Leon for his career in Japan.

Players of Asian descent change their names to Japanese names. (Many Koreans and Chinese, especially those born in Japan, do this to blend in with the Japanese and avoid prejudice.) Chunichi's ace stopper Kuo Yuan-tzu is known as Genji Kaku in Japan. After staying in Japan long enough, some Taiwanese have applied for permanent-residence status and been declared Japanese. The process is simpler if a player marries a Japanese woman, which is what Kaku did. He is now considered a Japanese, not a foreigner, and Chunichi is free to sign three other foreign players.

There is a particular problem identifying Taiwanese stars because most English-language dailies continue to refer to these players by their original names, not their Japanese names. Unless you follow Japanese baseball regularly, you'll be hard pressed to identify the Orions' Chuang Sheng-hsiung (Katsuo Soh) or the Lions' Kuo Tai-yuan (Taigen Kaku). The newspapers may be trying to be as unprejudiced as possible, but too often the system of double names ends up confusing fans.

Gaijin are often given uniforms with the numbers 4, 44, or 9. In the Japanese language, 4 is pronounced *shi,* and so is the word meaning death. The number 9 is pronounced *ku,* as is the word for pain. In much the same way that Westerners consider 13 unlucky, the Japanese distrust 4 and 9 and try to avoid them. But *gaijin* are thought immune to any ill effects of the superstition, and the numbers 4 and 9 can be put on their uniforms without danger.

Mainly hired as home-run hitters, *gaijin* have to get used to bizarre customs like being presented with a teddy bear or bouquet of flowers after they've rounded the bases. Awaiting them in front of the dugout is the entire team lined up to high-five away. The home-run welcoming celebration is a custom fit for a king.

Home runs are not the only thing *gaijin* are known for; they are also notorious for starting brawls after being hit by a pitch. These fights have produced some of the most hilarious scenes in Japanese ball. A 6′4″, 200-pound American batter charging the mound to punch the lights out of a 5′8″, 160-pound Japanese hurler invokes memories of Keystone Cop chases. The Japanese pitcher often hightails it for the outfield while the burly American gives chase. Taking a cue from the Americans, Japanese batters no longer grimace and bear it but charge the mound with as much gusto as the *gaijin*. Some irate Japanese batters have begun to employ creative tactics against the offending pitcher, things like a flying kung-fu leg kick or a rugby-style tackle.

Foreign players are never fully accepted in the world of Japanese baseball. In fact, a separate *gaijin* identity is promoted by the special treatment given foreign players. On the whole, foreigners do not follow the regimented training schedule that Japanese players do. Most can report to spring training in the spring, not on February 1. During the season, a foreign player's training is largely determined by the player himself. Starting pitchers are given four or five days' rest between starts and are not required to put in relief appearances or throw between innings or starts. Of course, there have been instances of clubs trying to force their methods on the reluctant foreign player, especially if he's in a slump. And a few players regularly attempt to assimilate by joining the Japanese in their bizarrely intense and long practice sessions, though sanity usually soon prevails.

Given this leeway in training and also the high salaries they command, foreigners are under intense pressure to perform well. Those who do not quickly adapt to the Japanese game and begin to play all-star-caliber ball almost immediately are benched or even sent home in midseason. Players are sometimes cut quite out of the blue.

Larry Parrish of the Yakult Swallows led the Central League in home runs his first season in Japan but found himself unemployed the following year. Between seasons Yakult had hired a new manager, Katsuya Nomura, who felt the club needed a *gaijin* outfielder who could supply power and speed. Parrish, an all-star at first base (but an outfielder in the Majors for part of his career), was cut from the squad to make room for a *gaijin* outfielder. Yakult lamely attempted to trade Parrish to the Pacific League but his high salary saw no takers. In reality, other teams probably colluded so as not to embarrass the Swallows on the bizarre decision to get rid of their leading home-run hitter. Eventually the Hanshin Tigers signed Parrish, getting the talented player for nothing, just after their own slugger, Cecil Fielder, had departed for the Detroit Tigers. The ironic thing is that Fielder left Hanshin because he saw how Parrish was having difficulty signing a second contract despite having an excellent first season in Japan.

Never really given a full shot in the Majors, Fielder came to Japan and promptly hit 38 home runs, despite a late-season injury that probably cost him the home-run title. The following year the Detroit Tigers offered Fielder a contract, and the rest is history. Fielder proceeded to hit 51 round-trippers, becoming the first American Leaguer in almost 30 years to hit more than 50 home runs. Fielder attributes his Major League success to the opportunity of getting to play regularly in Japan, experience he feels boosted his confidence. He also says he learned to be a more patient batter, as Japanese pitchers tend to throw more breaking balls than Major Leaguers do. Following his spectacular season with Detroit, Fielder returned on the 1990 Major League all-stars' tour of Japan and was easily the most popular player on the squad, as the Japanese heartily welcomed back their newly successful adopted son.

Despite the bizarre treatment players like Parrish have gotten, *gaijin* continue to flourish and star in Japan. One of the biggest in stardom and girth was Boog Powell-like first baseman Randy Bass of the Hanshin Tigers. Bass won back-to-back Triple Crowns and was the Series MVP when the Hanshin Tigers finally won their first Japan Series ever, but the Randy Bass story did not have a happy ending.

In 1988, which proved to be Bass' final season in Japan, his eight-year-old son had to return to the United States for a brain-tumor operation. Bass accompanied his son, staying with him throughout the trying time. Unfortunately it was the middle of baseball season and the Hanshin Tigers desperately needed Bass in the lineup. In Japanese companies, employees are rarely allowed time off for family illnesses, and the Tigers' management sent chief executive officer Shingo Furuya to the U.S. to persuade Bass to return to the playing field. But nothing Furuya said could change Bass' mind, as he refused to leave his son until the boy's condition stabilized.

Returning to Japan, Furuya felt so distraught at his failure to get Bass back that he committed suicide by jumping from his hotel-room balcony. Bass was eventually released by the Tigers and never returned to Japan as a player. Thankfully this case is the exception rather than the norm in Japanese baseball.

Another Bass-like first baseman, Boomer Wells of the Hankyu Braves, won the Triple Crown in 1984. The Giants' Warren Cromartie flirted with a .400 average for most of 1989, eventually ending up batting champion with a .378 average and leading the Giants to a Japan Series title. Cromartie was famous for his colorful home-run trot, during which he punched the air as the ball cleared the fence.

But it is not just on the playing field that a foreigner can make a positive contribution to Japanese baseball. Bill Gullickson pitched for the Giants for two years, during which time he wrote a book dealing with his affliction with diabetes. Gullickson donated all the royalties from the book to the Japan Diabetes Association. The association was so moved by the pitcher's generosity that it set up an annual "Gullickson Award" essay contest for young diabetes patients. Gullickson's short stay in Japan has left a lifelong legacy that truly stretches beyond the little white lines that frame the baseball diamond.

The Lee brothers played in Japan a combined 21 seasons and left their mark in the record book. Leon smacked 268 home runs and has a career batting average of .308, while Leron hit an all-time *gaijin* record of 283 home runs and holds a career batting average of .320.

Wally Yonamine played in Japan 12 years and was a three-time batting champion with the 1950s Giants. This Honolulu-born Japanese-American is generally credited with introducing "hustle" to Japanese baseball with his aggressive running style. His accomplishments are all the more noteworthy as he came to Japan in 1951, when second-generation Japanese were still viewed as war traitors. Able to endure the taunts of hecklers, Yonamine became a star player and later a talented coach and manager. In 1974 he piloted the Chunichi Dragons to the pennant, finally breaking the Giants' nine-year hold on the flag.

One *gaijin senshu* is even in the Japanese Baseball Hall of Fame. Victor Starfin, whose family had fled Russia after the Russian Revolution, grew up playing baseball in Hokkaido, Japan's northernmost island. After high school, Starfin went on to the pros, eventually becoming the first pitcher in Japan to win 300 games.

Of all the clubs, the Kintetsu Buffaloes seem to have the best luck signing foreign players. Kintetsu's *gaijin* have included two-time batting champion Jack Bloomfield in the early 1960s; two-time home-run leaders Clarence Jones in the mid 1970s and Charlie Manuel in the late 1970s; and in the 1980s and '90s slugger Ralph Bryant, always a league leader in home runs and RBIs. Bryant was plucked from the depths of the Chunichi Dragons' farm team and spirited away to star with Kintetsu. In 1989 he was named Pacific League MVP, while Warren Cromartie was named Central League MVP, the first time two *gaijin* had won the award in the same season.

At awards time many *gaijin* feel slighted. Some examples are simply cases of sour grapes but a very real problem is the all-star selection process. Just as there can be no more than two foreigners on a team at one time, there can be only two foreign players on the midyear and end-of-the-season all-star squads. Some seasons the top three or four spots in the home-run chase are held by foreign players, but when all-star time comes around, some of these players are left off the team. The process is blatantly unfair, as the all-star squads omit deserving foreigners and include lesser talented Japanese players. Also notorious are the player-of-the-week awards, rarely awarded to a *gaijin* two weeks in a row even if that player is the obvious choice.

Gaijin also feel slighted when they are approaching Japanese records. In 1985 Randy Bass was only one home run away from tying Sadaharu Oh's single-season record of 55 home runs. In the season's final game between Bass' Tigers and the Giants, then managed by Oh, the Giants' pitchers never gave Bass a chance to tie the record. They deliberately pitched around Bass every time he came to bat, despite the fact that the game did not call for walking him intentionally.

Foreign players cry foul at this gamesmanship but it is not directed only against *gaijin*. In 1988 two Japanese ballplayers on different clubs were battling for the batting crown. Lotte's Hideaki Takazawa sat out the season's final series against the Hankyu Braves with a league-leading .327 average. His rival, the Braves' Hiromi Matsunaga, closed to within .001 of Takazawa's average after a single in his first two at bats. Matsunaga was then walked 11 consecutive times during the remainder of the series, as the Lotte pitchers contrived to give their teammate the batting title.

Sadly this unfair play rears its head in the Majors too. In the famous National League home-run battle of 1929, Mel Ott of the New York Giants trailed the Phillies' Chuck Klein by just one home run during the last game of the season. But Ott never got a chance to take the crown. The Phillies' pitchers walked him every time he came up to the plate, thus handing the title to Klein.

And it isn't just the dark past that has seen tainted

batting titles. In 1976 the Royals' George Brett beat teammate Hal McRae and won the American League batting title by hitting a dubious single his last time at bat. The hit was a fly ball that landed safely in front of the Twins' Steve Brye when Brye made just a token effort to catch a very catchable ball. Interviewed after the game, Brye meekly denied that he had failed to hustle on the play and then suggested that Brett was more deserving of the title because he played a regular position, third base, while McRae was just a designated hitter.

Japanese baseball has a few records that foreign players will likely hold in perpetuity; these are the strike-out records. Most *gaijin* are signed on as sluggers, and by definition sluggers strike out more often than other batters. For example, Reggie Jackson, sixth on the Major Leagues' all-time home-run list, holds the dubious honor of being the all-time whiff artist too. With every yin there's a yang, and *gaijin* home-run hitters hold most of the strike-out records in Japanese baseball. Over the years the strike-out leaders may change but almost always they have foreign names.

Striking out can be an occupational hazard, as an unproductive *gaijin* is often made the scapegoat for a team's failure. *Gaijin* are easy targets, as few speak Japanese and even fewer stay around in the off season or for more than a few seasons. With their high salaries and sometimes very spacious homes, *gaijin* naturally tend to elicit resentful feelings. On any club there's always envy of a player making more money than his teammates, especially when the club is floundering. It is at such times that a foreign player's mental state is most severely tested. He may be forced to toe the line and train harder than he ever did in the Majors, or he may have to endure being put in and pulled out of the lineup according to nothing more than the manager's hunches.

The problem is sometimes not the player's fault at all. Trouble can start when a team does improper scouting and signs a player unfit for the role he is expected to assume. On various occasions, Japanese clubs have signed infielders (who usually hit for average) and expected them to become home-run hitters practically overnight. A player used to leading off in the Majors ends up batting third or cleanup in Japan, and the Japanese wonder why he can't perform the Ruthian task he's been assigned.

Then there is the infamous matter of the expanding strike zone. Too many foreign ballplayers have noticed that the strike zone becomes bigger the more successful they are in Japan. In a sense, the expanding strike zone is the great leveler in Japanese baseball. Umpires begin to be less than fair with foreign players, and a kind of Japanese group collusion exists to try to limit a foreigner's success. The foreign player is allowed to be good but not too good, as that would show up the Japanese. This situation has improved immensely over the years but old habits die hard and the expanding strike zone refuses to disappear. Those foreign players who can swallow their pride and become immune to the frustrations are the ones who succeed in Japan.

Despite all the hassles that foreign ballplayers bring to the Japanese game, *gaijin* continue to be signed to contracts because they win games! One of the most outstanding foreign players was Joe Stanka, a gutsy, hard-throwing pitcher who fit the American stereotype of belligerence and hard-nosed play. Stanka's Don Drysdale, stick-it-in-your-ear pitching style won him few fans but in 1964 he ended up the Japan Series MVP, pitching three shutouts and leading the Nankai Hawks over the

Hanshin Tigers in a seven-game thriller. The ace of the staff, Stanka was a remarkable 26 and 7 on the season.

Astute *gaijin* signings can put more people in the stands. When Bob Horner was signed by the Yakult Swallows in 1987, "Hornermania" gripped the Japanese baseball world. Horner, an often injured infielder for the Atlanta Braves, passed up an unsatisfactory contract offer from Atlanta and jumped to Japan for the season. Not signed until the season was well under way, Horner hit 31 home runs in just 93 games. His debut in Japanese baseball was probably the most spectacular of any *gaijin* star. For once the Japanese could see a bona fide Major Leaguer in his prime. That year the crowds flocking to Yakult Swallows' games were not there to see a club playing under .500 ball; they were there to see Horner. After such an impressive first season, he was offered one of the biggest contracts ever presented a foreign player. But 1988 saw Horner in the uniform of the St. Louis Cardinals as, love it or leave it, Japan is not the land of Major League baseball. Despite his success in Japan's ballparks, Horner yearned to return to America and his own culture.

Horner and his *gaijin senshu* colleagues are de facto baseball mercenaries. They arrive in Japan for the adventure and the money but the Majors is still *the* place to play baseball. In addition, the benefits of playing in Japan are outweighed by the difficulties of bridging the cultural gaps between the home country and Japan. Meanwhile, the three-player limit on foreigners keeps the number of *gaijin* manageable for the Japanese baseball establishment; of more than 200 professional ballplayers in Japan, only 36, at most, are foreigners. The different numbers and unusual names given foreigners emphasize the marginal position that *gaijin* occupy in the

Japanese baseball community. Though there have been a few exceptions, most foreigners who survive the pressures of life in a foreign country, the expanding strike zone, teammates' envy of their high salaries, etc., do not remain in Japan very long. Sad but true, the star of the typical *gaijin senshu* burns like a comet, bright with a short life span, then crashes down to earth.

7

TOURS

A HIGHLIGHT OF many baseball seasons in Japan is the arrival of the Major Leaguers, who periodically cross the Pacific to let the local heroes test their mettle against the best from the West. The Japanese have long taken these games very seriously, while the Major Leaguers have tended to view the postseason tour as a paid vacation. These are, after all, just exhibition games.

Even before there was professional baseball in Japan, various foreign teams toured the country under different auspices. The first tour was in 1908 by a team called the Reach All-Americans, a group of minor and Major League players put together by the A. J. Reach sporting-goods company. (Could this have possibly started the thinking that led to direct corporate sponsorship of Japanese professional teams?) There was even a tour by the Black Royal Giants of the Negro League, when American baseball was still separated along racial lines.

The Black Royal Giants won 23 games and tied one on that tour.

Before 1950, when Japan's two professional leagues were established, the tours pitted American professional players against Japanese amateur sides made up chiefly of college players. Matched against professionals, the Japanese amateurs were slaughtered, winning just two games out of the 135 played between 1908 and 1934. The 1931 Major League squad included Yankee great Lou Gehrig, and Babe Ruth was a member of the team in 1934. The Bambino's popularity bridged the Pacific Ocean and helped spawn the idea that Japan too should have baseball at the professional level.

A story revealed years later was that the 1934 Major League squad included a spy! Moe Berg, a noted linguist and scholar, also happened to be a Major League catcher and spy for the U.S. government. According to his biography, Berg pretended to be visiting a patient in a Tokyo hospital but was actually filming the city skyline from the hospital rooftop. His films were later used by the military to plan bombing raids on Tokyo during World War II. Who says that politics and sports don't mix!

After World War II, Japan's professionals pulled themselves out from under the ashes of destruction and by 1949 were ready to face the Pacific Coast League's San Francisco Seals. But the Japanese pros fared little better than their amateur predecessors, losing all seven games to the AAA-level Seals.

In 1951 the Major League tour was led by Lefty O'Doul, who had previously brought pro teams from the U.S. and was on his way to becoming America's unofficial baseball ambassador to Japan. During that tour the Major Leaguers lost their first game ever but finished with 13 wins, one loss, and two ties. This time Yankee great Joe DiMaggio was on board for a last hurrah before retiring from the game.

Since that time teams have usually toured every two years or so. The Japanese pros even soundly beat one National League team! In 1970 the San Francisco Giants finished their tour with three wins and six losses. The tour took place in March, as the Giants had agreed to hold part of their spring training in Japan. Despite the presence of future Hall of Famers Willie Mays, Willie McCovey, and Juan Marichal, the team was not in shape or as sharp as it should have been. The Giants simply used the Japan tour to prepare for the season ahead, not to try to prove anything against the Japanese.

Recent tours have featured Major Leaguers from various teams, but most early tours consisted of games between a Major League team and one Japanese club, or a Major League club and a Japanese all-star squad. Because individual teams tended to lose to the Major Leaguers, they sometimes combined teams in hopes of defeating the common foe. In 1978 the Cincinnati Reds played a total of 17 games, nine against the Yomiuri Giants, two against Japanese all-stars, and the rest against a Giants' squad with players recruited from cities where the games were held. For example, for a game in Osaka the Giants were joined by players from the Nankai Hawks and the Kintetsu Buffaloes. The different teams made little difference to Cincinnati, however, as the Big Red Machine steamrollered all the opposition it faced, finishing with 14 wins, two losses, and one tie.

The Yomiuri Giants have always been the driving force behind the Major League tours, a legacy from founder Matsutaro Shoriki, who dreamed of a true "world series" between the Japanese champion and the Major League champion. As the Giants were molded into champions, Shoriki intended for his beloved team to be given the opportunity to challenge for the "world series." The closest the Giants came to facing an elite team was in 1971, when the Baltimore Orioles, the reigning American League champions, toured Japan. The Orioles proceeded to wallop the Giants, winning eight games, tying three, and losing just one. A true "world series" was still a long way off.

An important change occurred in 1988, when an all-star squad led by Sparky Anderson scraped through with just three wins, two losses, and two ties. For once there was little talk about the Major Leaguers' superiority and a lot of talk about the improved play of the Japanese.

Before the 1988 tour began, all attention was focused on Dodger pitcher Orel Hershiser, coming off a World Series championship and a season in which he broke Don Drysdale's record for consecutive scoreless innings pitched. Against the Japanese, Hershiser got bombed in the seven or so innings he pitched. Due to the layoff after the World Series, Hershiser was obviously off form; and like all the Major League players, he treated the series as a postseason vacation rather than an important baseball experience. Plaudits for the 1988 tour went to Hiromi Makihara, the Giants' pitcher who struck out nine Major League hitters over nine innings.

In 1990 the seemingly impossible happened when the Japanese all-stars took the series by beating a combined Major League squad four games to three, with one tie thrown in for good measure. The tour included a combined no-hitter by California Angel Chuck Finley and Seattle Mariner Randy Johnson in the final game. But the real story of the tour was the play of the Japanese, who reeled off four straight victories before the Major Leaguers could break into the victory column. For once the hitting of the Japanese kept pace with their fairly solid pitching. Heroes of the tour were Daiei Hawk Makoto Sasaki, who hit .409, and Seibu Lion Koji Akiyama, whose base stealing and center-field defense were new sides of the slugger's ability.

The 1990 tour proved that no longer can the Major Leaguers bring less than their best to play against the Japanese. (Stars like Dwight Gooden, Will Clark, Ryne Sandberg, Jose Canseco, and Rickey Henderson were missing from the 1990 tour.) Jet lag and the month-long layoff cannot be cited as excuses for the Major Leaguers' losses, since other squads played (and won!) under similar circumstances. The truth is that Japanese players have improved their game considerably, and the time has come for a legitimate series pitting the best players from Japan against the best from North America.

Though the current setup generates considerable interest in Japan, it is hardly an ideal arrangement. Holding the games after the Japan Series is a disadvantage to the Major Leaguers, who with a month's vacation are already out of their groove and perhaps out of shape too. Playing all games in Japan is another unfair advantage for the Japanese.

A solution to these problems would be to play a number of games in North America during the actual season, though this plan presents various logistical difficulties. Still, there is a precedent for such a series in the sports world. Soviet hockey teams manage to play a number of exhibition games against North American pro teams during the regular season, and baseball teams could do the same. In any case, though they have taken just one series from the Major Leaguers, the Japanese players have earned the right to play the big boys at their Big League parks.

This is not to say that Japanese baseball is as good as Major League ball; there are still plenty of weak areas in the Japanese game. A key to improving the Japanese level of play is to release the stranglehold the leagues, clubs, press, and fans have on their heroes. If top Japanese stars want to go to North America to become better players, they should be encouraged. The presence of Latin players in the Majors has been beneficial to all concerned. North America already provides opportunities for top-class Europeans to excel in basketball, hockey, and other sports. It is time for Japanese baseball to follow suit. Only by playing with and against the best can Japanese players raise their game to the world-class level.

Such thinking has led the Seibu Lions to loan out their farm-squad players to the A-level San Jose (California) Bees for seasoning. The thinking is that by competing against future Major Leaguers, young Japanese will more quickly develop the skills that make them complete ballplayers. A successful example of the process is Seibu shortstop Norio Tanabe, who spent a season in the California sun rather than ride the pine with the parent club in Japan or play in the weak Japanese minor league. After a fine season with the San Jose Bees, hitting .312 in 140 games (ten more than the Japanese schedule), Tanabe was recalled to Japan. Within two seasons he was a regular in the Lions' lineup.

The Salinas (California) Spurs, another A-level club, even have a Japanese manager, Hidehiko Koga. Koga has managed and coached in both Japan and North America since the 1960s, and began managing Salinas in 1990. Twelve Japanese players are regularly on the Spurs' roster.

Technology could play an important part in determining the future of Japanese baseball. With satellite and cable television slowly gaining ground in Japan, Major League games are being regularly broadcast into people's homes. It is possible that comparisons between Japanese baseball and Major League baseball will increase, and Japanese fans will begin to demand better baseball. Or possibly the Majors' brand of ball will become a cult sport followed by expats and a few Japanese armchair baseball junkies.

Ultimately the impact of the Major Leagues may be limited to the fashion front. Japanese young people, preoccupied with Americana, will likely continue to adorn themselves in Phillies caps, Yankees warmup jackets, and whatever else strikes their fancy. Paradoxically, Japanese baseball may continue to shun the Major Leagues' methods and stick to the tried and true, safety-first baseball.

For some deluded members of the Japanese baseball establishment, future victories over the Major Leaguers may vindicate Japanese baseball's traditional methods. The only way to settle the "who's best" argument is to hold a true world championship series that features the top clubs of the top baseball areas—Cuba, Japan, and North America. Despite the hoopla that accompanies an exhibition series, the games are meaningless without something at stake on both sides of the diamond.

The tours will likely continue, drawing crowds at less than capacity, as interest in these encounters is tailing off. The truth is that by November when the Major Leaguers arrive in Japan, the Japanese fan has overdosed on baseball. Still, the tours have a redeeming factor, in that they give Japanese fans a chance to see Major League stars in person. The flair, excitement, and sheer fun the Major Leaguers bring to the ballpark are things the Japanese ball fan can enjoy on any level, whether Japanese teams are competitive or not.

▲ This scoreboard is fairly typical of scoreboards
in Japan but the tower in the background
marks the site as Nagoya Stadium.

▲ Shigeo Nagashima, "Mr. Giants," is the most
popular Japanese ballplayer of all time. Today his
face can be seen and his voice heard on countless television programs.

► The immortal Sadaharu Oh works on his
batting form.

► A sumo wrestler tries his hand at the ceremonial first pitch.

▼ Hiromitsu Ochiai stares in disbelief after he's struck out. Not many pitches get by Ochiai, Japan's only three-time Triple Crown winner.

► "Tiger! Tiger! burning bright . . ." Cecil
Fielder as a Hanshin Tiger tries to swat
another home run.

◄ With his unique windup, Kintetsu's Hideo Nomo is about to launch a blazing fastball homeward.

▲ Warren Cromartie of the Giants participates in the "hero interview" after another starring performance. The man on the right is an interpreter.

8

JAPLISH

As BASEBALL ORIGINATED in the United States, many of the baseball terms you hear in Japan are Japanized forms of English words. Tune in any TV broadcast and you'll hear the announcers talking about the *pitchā* (pitcher) and the *battā* (batter), a *pinchi hittā* (pinch hitter) and a *pinchi rannā* (pinch runner). It was not always this way.

In the years preceding and during World War II, Japan's government wanted to expunge the national language of "Japlish," Japanized versions of English words. Genuine Japanese equivalents like *tōshu* and *dasha* replaced "corrupting" Japlish terms like *pitchā* and *battā*.

Even teams were forced to change their names. A team previously called the Eagles became Kurowashi, Japanese for eagle. Other clubs dropped their former names entirely, adopting a new moniker. The Osaka Tigers took on the company name, Hanshin (though they reverted to the Osaka Tigers after the war). During the insular period, everything from stationery letterheads to team uniforms was cleansed of foreignness and changed to Japanese.

Once peace returned to Japan, the baseball moguls quickly switched back to calling a pitcher *pitchā,* a tradition that still holds true. Some of the Japlish terms used today are quite close to the original English terms; others almost require a degree in linguistics to understand. Following are some of the most commonly used examples of baseball Japlish; information about words' origins appears within parentheses.

abekku hōmuran (*avec* home run; literally a "with home run," *avec* being French for with) a pair of home runs hit by a team's top two batters

ahō kōru (*ahō* call; literally an idiot call, *ahō* being Japanese for idiot) a call yelled by fans dissatisfied with a player's, manager's, or umpire's performance

anchi kyojin (anti *kyojin*) anti-Giants' sentiment or a person who strongly dislikes the Giants

appā suingu (upper swing) an uppercut swing. The opposite down swing is pronounced *daun suingu.*

arupusu sutando (Alps stand) a famous section of Koshien Stadium that is likened to the Alps because of its steep rise

auto an out. *auto, auto* is often sarcastically yelled by fans to mock an opposing batter who makes an out.

bakku netto (back net) the back screen behind home plate that protects spectators from foul balls

bakku sukuriin (back screen) dead center field. The area beyond the center-field fence usually has a scoreboard or screen. The *bakku sukuriin* home run is Japanese baseball's most spectacular hit.

batafurai bōru (butterfly ball) a super slow pitch that gently floats toward home plate

battā a batter

battā bokkusu a batter's box

battingu sutansu a batting stance

battingu tōshu a batting-practice pitcher. The Japanese word for pitcher is *tōshu*.

batto a bat

bea guraundo (bare ground) an infield with no grass or artificial turf, e.g., Koshien Stadium's all-dirt infield

benchi repōtā (bench reporter) a commentator who sends periodic reports from the dugout during a broadcast

bēsubōru a baseball. The game of baseball is *yakyū*, literally field ball.

bēsurain a base line. Note that *bēsu* is not used to refer to the bases themselves. First base is *ichirui,* second base is *nirui,* and third is *sanrui.*

besuto nain   (best nine) an end-of-the-season all-star team, composed of nine players, one for each position on the field

beteran senshu   an experienced or veteran player. *senshu* means player or athlete.

bōru   a ball, as in one strike and two balls. Note that Japanese count strikes first and balls second.

buroku sain   (block sign) a sign given by a coach to a hitter, base runner, etc. The expression *konbinēshon sain* (combination sign) is also used.

chenji appu   a change-up (pitch)

chia gāru   (cheer girl) a female cheerleader

chia gurūpu   a cheerleading group or section

chiimu purē   (team play) teamwork. The term usually describes skillful fielding that results in a double play.

chūkei purē   (*chūkei* play) a cut-off play or throw

daburu heddā   a doubleheader. A doubleheader is a rare occurrence in Japanese baseball, usually scheduled only to make up a game that was rained out.

daiyamondo gurabu shō   (Diamond Glove *shō*) a fielding award, the equivalent of the Major Leagues' Gold Glove Award

deddo bōru (dead ball) a pitch that strikes a batter, sending him to first base. The term comes from the fact that once the ball strikes a batter it is dead, i.e., no longer in play.

dē gēmu a day game

doa suingu (door swing) a smooth swing (like a door opening in a smooth arc)

dorafuto ken a draft pick

dorō gēmu (draw game) a tie game

entaitoru tsū bēsu (entitled two base) a ground-rule double. When a hit ball bounces over an outfield fence, the batter is automatically awarded second base.

erā an error

fain purē (fine play) a nice (fielding) play

fāmu a farm club. The term *nigun* is also used.

fāsuto a first baseman or first base

fauru a foul ball

fensu an outfield fence

foa bōru (four balls) a walk. An intentional walk is *keien foa bōru*.

fōku bōru a forkball

furii battingu (free batting) batting practice

furu bēsu (full base) bases loaded. The term *manrui* is also used.

furu kaunto a full count, i.e., two strikes and three balls. The term *tsū surii* (two three) is also used.

gattsu pōzu (guts pose) a gesture to the fans, e.g., punching the air, made after a key play. Call it hot-dogging, showboating, or playing to the fans, the *gattsu pōzu* is becoming more and more a part of Japanese baseball.

gēmu sa (game *sa*) the number of games a team is behind the league leader in the standings

gēmu setto (game set) an expression commonly said by announcers after the final out of the game. The origin of the phrase is "game, set, and match" from tennis.

gettsū (get two) a double play. The fielders "get two" runners on the play. The term *daburu purē* is also used.

gisei furai (*gisei* fly) a sacrifice fly. A sacrifice bunt is a *gisei banto*.

goro a grounder. The term appears in combinations like

fasuto goro, a ground ball that is hit to the first baseman.

gurōbu   a glove

gyakuten chansu   a come-from-behind chance at taking the lead in a game. *gyakuten* means reversal, and in this phrase refers to the possibility that the score may be reversed at this point in the game.

hangā kābu   (hanger curve) a hanging curveball

heddo suraidingu   (head sliding) a headfirst slide into a base

herumetto   a (batting) helmet

hiirō intabyū   (hero interview) a postgame interview with the star of the game, usually held on a platform behind home plate, broadcast not only on TV but also inside the stadium

hitto endo ran   a hit-and-run play. The opposite is known as *ran endo hitto.*

hōmuin   (home in) a run. When a runner crosses the plate, the announcer says *hōmuin,* the equivalent of our expression "the runner comes home."

hōmuran   a home run. For statistics, the term *honrui* is used but TV commentators prefer the Japlish *hōmuran.*

jamingu   (jamming) spying on the catcher's signals from

the center-field bleachers and relaying the information to the dugout. The spy tries to disrupt (jam) the signal being relayed from catcher to pitcher. The practice is illegal.

jishū torēningu (*jishū* training) individual, off-season training. Management may "encourage" a player to train harder during the winter if he's had a subpar season.

katto ofu purē a cutoff play

kōchi a coach

kōchi bokkusu the coach's box down the first- and third-base lines. Next to home plate is the batter's box, *battā bokkusu*.

kondōmu fūsen (condom *fūsen*) a balloon (*fūsen*) released into the air in the seventh inning. Supposedly Hanshin Tigers' fans named the suspiciously shaped objects *kondōmu fūsen*.

kōrudo gēmu a game called because of rain, a time limit, an earthquake, etc.

kuriin appu torio a cleanup trio, featuring the number-three, number-four (*kuriin appu hittā*), and number-five hitters in the batting order

kuriin hitto (clean hit) a well-placed hit, usually a single, that goes through the infield without a fielder touching it *kyatchā* a catcher

kyatchi bōru (catch ball) the game of catch

kyanpu in (camp in) the official opening of spring training on February 1

manējā (manager) a club's traveling secretary. A club's
field manager is *kantoku*.

manrui hōmā a grand-slam home run. *manrui* means
bases loaded.

maundo the (pitching) mound

menyū (menu) a training schedule, e.g., light running,
followed by infield practice, then base running, etc.

mitto a (fielder's) mitt

mūdo mēkā (mood maker) a charismatic player able to
lift the spirits of the team

naisu kabā (nice cover) good backup play. For example, if the pitcher covers first base on a grounder hit
to the first baseman and the runner is put out, the
announcer will say *naisu kabā*.

naitā a night game

nekusuto battāzu sākuru (next batter's circle) the on-
deck circle. The term *uētingu sākuru* (waiting circle)
is also used.

nijū byō rūru a rule requiring the pitcher to complete a pitch within twenty seconds of receiving the ball from the catcher or infielder. The rule is largely ignored in Japan.

nokkā (knocker) a coach who hits (knocks) the ball for fielding practice

ōbii (O.B., an abbreviation of old boy) a former player or participant, known as an oldtimer in North America

ōpun sen (open *sen*) a spring exhibition game

pa riigu (*pa* league) the abbreviation for the Pacific League

pasu bōru (pass ball) a passed ball; a pitch that the catcher fails to catch, allowing the base runner to advance

pitchā purēto (pitcher plate) the pitching rubber, on which the pitcher must stand before beginning his windup

pitchingu fōmu pitching form or style

pitchingu sutaffu a pitching staff

pinchi hittā a pinch hitter

pinchi rannā a pinch runner

poketto kyatchi (pocket catch) a basket catch; a catch

made with the glove hand palmside up, with the glove used as a sort of basket

pōru (pole) a foul pole

purē bōru "Play ball!"

puro yakyū Japanese pro baseball

pusshu banto (push bunt) a bunt in which a right-handed batter tries to push the ball between the pitcher and the first baseman, or a left-handed batter tries to push the ball between the pitcher and the third baseman

rainā (liner) a line drive

rain appu a line-up

raito (right) right field or a right fielder

rakkii sebun (lucky seven) the seventh inning, during which fans try to inspire their team by cheering and releasing screeching balloons before the team comes to bat. Standing up and stretching your weary body during *rakkii sebun,* after sitting on a hard bleacher seat for six innings, is optional.

rakkii zōn (lucky zone) the gap between the outfield fence and the first row of bleachers. A ball hit into the *rakkii zōn* barely clears the fence but is "lucky" in that it is still a home run. At Koshien Stadium the bullpens are located in the *rakkii zōn.*

ranningu hōmā (running homer) an inside-the-park

home run. The Japanese term attests to the fact that the player must run, not trot, around the bases to beat the throw home.

refuto   (left) left field or a left fielder

refuto ōbā   (left over) a hit that flies over the left fielder's head. A *raito ōbā* (right over) passes over the right fielder's head and a *sentā ōbā* (center over) goes over the center fielder's head.

regāzu   (leg guards) the shin guards worn by a catcher

ririifu kā   (relief car) a car that transports the relief pitcher into the game from the bullpen to the pitcher's mound

sādo   third base or a third baseman

saikuru hitto   (cycle hit) four hits—a single, double, triple, and home run—in a single game. For base stealers, the *saikuru suchiiru* (cycle steal) consists of stealing second, third, and home in one game.

sain bōru   (sign ball) an autographed baseball

sain purē   (sign play) a signal made by a coach that calls for a certain play, pitch, etc. If a coach puts on the double-steal sign and the play comes off, an announcer will often praise the coach's *sain purē*.

sākasu purē   (circus play) a circus catch; a spectacular catch that usually ends with the fielder tumbling to the ground *sayōnara gēmu* (*sayōnara* game) the last game in a veteran player's career or the last game of the season. A *sayōnara hōmā* (*sayōnara* homer) is a game-winning home run in the last at-bat for the home team, and a *sayōnara hitto* is a game-winning hit in the last at-bat. A *sayōnara chansu* is the last at-bat chance to win the game.

sēbu a save

sēfutii banto (safety bunt) a bunt in which the hitter tries to get on base rather than send a runner to second or third. The term *doraggu banto* (drag bunt) is also used.

sēfutii sukuiizu (safety squeeze) a play in which a runner on third base starts for home after seeing how the batter bunts the ball. In a *suisaido sukuiizu* (suicide squeeze) the runner breaks for home before seeing how or if the ball is bunted.

sekando second base or a second baseman

sentā center field or a center fielder

sentā furai (center fly) a fly ball to center field. A *raito furai* goes to right field, and a *refuto furai* goes to left.

sentā mae a hit that lands in front (*mae*) of the center fielder. A *raito mae* lands in front of the right fielder and a *refuto mae* lands in front of the left fielder.

se riigu (*se* league) the abbreviation for the Central League *shadō pitchingu* (shadow pitching) pitching practice without a ball. For other players, there's *shadō purei,* which is batting, fielding, or throwing practice without a ball.

shiisō gēmu (seesaw game) a tight contest in which the lead changes hands throughout the game

shiizun ofu (season off) the off-season

shinboru māku (symbol mark) a logo

shōto a shortstop

shūki kyanpu (*shūki* camp) autumn training

shūto (shoot) a screwball pitch that due to its spin "shoots" toward home plate

suitchi hittā a switch-hitter

sukoa bōdo a scoreboard

sukoa bukku a scorebook

supaiku (spike) a baseball shoe with spikes

supurē dahō (spray *dahō*) spray hitting; hitting to all fields

supuritto fingā fāsuto bōru a split-finger fastball

suraidā a slider

suta men   (shortened form of "starting member") a starting lineup

sutando purē   (stand play) a stand-up cheer led by cheerleaders

sute gēmu   a meaningless game, usually near the end of the season, when also-rans play each other

sutoraiku   a strike

sutorēto   a straight fastball

tatchi appu   (touch up) tagging up on a fly ball and advancing to the next base

tatchi auto   (touch out) tagged out

taimurii tsū bēsu   (timely two base) a timely double. Any run-scoring hit can be referred as a *taimurii hitto*.

tekisasu hitto   (Texas hit) a short fly that lands beyond the infielders' reach. English equivalents include a Texas leaguer, a bloop single, and a dying quail.

tosu battingu   (toss batting) a pepper game; a kind of batting practice in which a coach lightly tosses the ball perhaps three feet to the side of the player. The drill is intended to improve timing and rhythm.

uesuto bōru   (waste ball) a wasted pitch; a pitch purposely thrown out of the strike zone that the pitcher hopes the batter will swing at *uiningu sumairu* (winning smile) the expression the winning pitcher has on his face after the game

wairudo pitchi a wild pitch

yūshō pātii (*yūshō* party) a victory party, usually a wild affair with sprayed beer, that follows the clinching of a pennant. A *yūshō parēdo* is a victory parade through the streets of the city.

Not all Japanese baseball terms are Japlish; some are genuine Japanese words. You're bound to catch some of the following on almost any broadcast.

anda a base hit

bōgyoritsu earned run average; ERA

daritsu batting average

dasha a batter

daten run(s) batted in; RBI

gaiyashu an outfielder

hesatsu a double play

hoshu a catcher

ichiban dasha a leadoff hitter

ichiruishu a first baseman

kai an inning

kantoku a manager

kyūen tōshu a relief pitcher

naiya anda an infield hit

naiyashu an infielder

niruishu a second baseman

omote the top half of an inning

sanruishu a third baseman

sanshin a strikeout

senshu a player

shikyū a walk

shimei dasha a designated hitter; DH

shinpan an umpire

shubi bōgai interference

shubi renshū fielding practice

sokyū a fastball

tokuten a run

tōkyū pitching

tōkyū renshūjo a bullpen

tōrui a stolen base

tōshu a pitcher

ura the bottom half of an inning

yashu sentaku a fielder's choice

yūgekishu a shortstop

Baseball is baseball, so you're bound to understand

the game even if you don't speak a word of Japanese. But knowing just a bit of the language can increase your understanding of Japanese baseball (and perhaps of the Japanese people too). If you're really lucky, you may see an exciting game that goes into *enchō sen* (extra innings) and is decided by a *sayōnara hōmā,* with the winning pitcher throwing a *muandajiai* (no-hitter). Weirder things have happened, and after all this is Japanese baseball.

9

TICKETS AND MEDIA

BUYING TICKETS TO a ballgame in Japan is fairly easy and straightforward. Don't be put off by possible language problems; just follow the signs and step right up.

First off, decide where you want to sit. This is easy because Japanese baseball parks are fairly uniform. Most stadiums have just one deck, so there's no need to worry that you'll be in the nosebleed section if you make a mistake. The following terms cover most seating sections:

bleachers *gaiya* 外野
left- or right-field line *naiya* 内野
infield seat B *shiito*/C *shiito* Bシート/Cシート
best seat (behind home plate) A *shiito* Aシート

If you want a reserved seat, ask for *shitei seki;* for an unreserved seat, ask for *jiyū seki.* Usually the bleachers and the infield corners are unreserved, though Tokyo

Dome and Jingu Stadium recently put plastic reserved-seating sections in the front half of the bleachers. Despite similarities among the various stadiums, each has its own seating intricacies, briefly described in the following paragraphs:

Fujiidera Stadium (Kintetsu Buffaloes)
(0729) 39-5775

"Special seats" are box seats. A seats lie to either side of the "special seats." B seats are behind and above the A seats.

NEAREST STATION: Fujiidera on the Kintetsu Line.

Green Stadium Kobe (Orix BlueWave)
(078) 794-2511

Box seats are directly behind home plate in the first level. A seats lie to either side of the boxes in the first level, extending to the first- and third-base bags. A seats also stretch from home to first and from home to third in the second level. B seats run down the lines and wrap around the foul poles.

NEAREST STATION: Sogo Undo Koen on the Seishin subway line.

Heiwadai Stadium (Fukuoka Daiei Hawks)
(092) 781-2153

A and B seats wrap around either side of the season-ticket boxes. Unreserved infield seats make up almost half of the seating in foul territory (unlike at other parks, where most seats in foul territory are reserved).

NEAREST STATIONS: Akasaka and Ohari Koen on the Fukuoka subway line. Look for the moat by the side of Meiji-dori, Meiji Street, and you'll find the stadium.

Hiroshima Civic Stadium (Hiroshima Toyo Carp)
(082) 228-5291

A seats are on either side of the box seats in the first deck and directly behind home plate in the second deck. B seats are in the upper deck down the lines.

NEAREST STATIONS: From JR Hiroshima Station, take a streetcar and get off at either Genbaku (A-bomb) Domu-mae or at Kamiya-cho. Genbaku Domu-mae will put you directly in front of the stadium, while Kamiya-cho is about a two-minute walk away. Most streetcars stop at both stops.

Jingu Stadium (Yakult Swallows)
(03) 3404-8999

A small second deck behind home plate has A and B seats. The infield seats become higher-priced seats for games against the Giants.

NEAREST STATIONS: Gaien-mae on the Ginza Line and Sendagaya on the Sobu Line. Gaien-mae is much closer, just a five-minute walk from the stadium.

Kawasaki Stadium (Lotte Orions)
(044) 244-1171

Box seats called "season seats" are sold on a season-ticket basis. A seats higher up behind home plate and infield seats down the lines are available. Lotte's tickets are the cheapest in Japanese baseball.

NEAREST STATIONS: Keikyu Kawasaki (also called Kei-hin Kawasaki) on the Keihin Kyuko Line and Kawasaki on the Tokaido Line. To get to the stadium, exit Kawasaki Station, walk straight up the main street, Shiyakusho-dori, about eight minutes, and you'll see the ballpark on your right.

Koshien Stadium (Hanshin Tigers)
(0798) 47-1041
Box seats are in the first level only. In the second level, green seats are behind home plate, yellow seats are behind first base, and orange seats are behind third base. A seats are located in the third level. The infield seats down the left-field line become more expensive for games against the Giants. The famous "Alps stand" is down the right-field line.

NEAREST STATION: Koshien on the Hanshin Line, between Osaka and Kobe.

Nagoya Stadium (Chunichi Dragons)
(052) 351-5171
Green, red, and yellow seats are sold on a season-ticket basis. Orange seats are down the base lines. Blue seats are down the left- and right-field lines.

NEAREST STATIONS: JR Nagoya Kyujo Shomen and Nagoya Kyujo-mae on the Meitetsu Line, both ten or fifteen minutes from Nagoya Station. The JR station, open only on game days, is a tad closer to the ballpark.

Seibu Lions Stadium (Seibu Lions)
(0429) 25-1151
All box seats are sold on a season-ticket basis. In the rest of the stadium are both reserved and unreserved infield and bleacher seats.

NEAREST STATION: Seibu Kyujo-mae on the Seibu Shinjuku and the Seibu Ikebukuro lines. Check the train schedule carefully; not all trains go directly to the stadium.

Tokyo Dome (Yomiuri Giants/Nippon Ham Fighters)
(03) 3811-2111
At Giants' games only, S seats are box seats. At both

teams' games, A seats are in the first and second decks down the first- and third-base lines. B seats are in all decks; in the third deck they lie right behind home plate. C seats are in the third deck and in the corners of the second deck.

NEAREST STATIONS: Korakuen on the Marunouchi Line, which stops across the street from the bleacher entrance, and Suidobashi on the Sobu Line, which stops on the opposite side of the Dome.

Yokohama Stadium (Yokohama Taiyo Whales)
(045) 661-1251
A seats are down the lines, as are B seats, which curl around the foul poles.

NEAREST STATIONS: Kannai on the Keihin Tohoku-Negishi Line and Kannai on the Yokohama subway line.

Once you arrive at a stadium, you'll need to find the right ticket booth. The ticket booth for the bleacher section is directly behind the bleachers. The ticket booth for box seats is located toward the main entrance to the stadium. Don't hesitate to ask anyone who looks even vaguely like an official for help.

For most games it's fairly easy to purchase tickets on the day of the game. Exceptions are all Giants' games and games on weekends or national holidays, all of which can be sellouts.

All stadiums have advance tickets (*mae uri*) on sale at their main ticket booth, usually beginning two to three weeks prior to the scheduled home stand. You can find out who's playing on a particular day by checking that day's English-language newspaper.

Obtain free pocket schedules by going to stadium

booths or by writing to the clubs themselves at the following addresses:

Chunichi Dragons
Chunichi Bldg. 9F
4-1-11 Sakae, Naka-ku
Nagoya 460

Fukuoka Daiei Hawks
Otemon Pine Bldg. 6F
1-1-12 Otemon, Chuo-ku
Fukuoka 810

Hanshin Tigers
1-47 Koshien-cho
Nishinomiya-shi
Hyogo-ken 663

Hiroshima Toyo Carp
Hiroshima Shimin Kyujo
5-25 Motomachi, Naka-ku
Hiroshima 730

Kintetsu Buffaloes
Kintetsu Namba Bldg. 7F
4-1-15 Namba, Chuo-ku
Osaka 542

Lotte Orions
2-2-33 Hyakunin-cho
Shinjuku-ku
Tokyo 169

Nippon Ham Fighters
Roppongi Denki Bldg. 6F
6-1-20 Roppongi, Minato-ku
Tokyo 106

Orix BlueWave
Kanri Center 2F
Midoridai, Suma-ku
Kobe 654-01

Seibu Lions
Seibu Lions Kyujo
2135 Kami-yamaguchi
Tokorozawa-shi
Saitama-ken 359

Yakult Swallows
Yakult Bldg. 7F
1-1-19 Higashi-shimbashi, Minato-ku
Tokyo 105

Yokohama Taiyo Whales
Kinoshita Shoji Bldg. 7F
4-43 Masago-cho, Naka-ku
Yokohama 231

Yomiuri Giants
1-3-7 Uchikanda, Chiyoda-ku
Tokyo 101

Your best bet for obtaining tickets may be the many
ticket centers in cities where teams are located. Main
ticket centers include the following:

Tickets for TOKYO DOME and JINGU STADIUM

Shinjuku	Isetan Playguide (03) 3352-1111
	My City Ticket Bureau (03) 3352-1521
	Ticket Saison (Jingu only) (03) 3354-0141
Shibuya	Tokyu Ticket Center (03) 3406-1513
	Ticket Saison (Jingu only) (03) 3462-3708
Ikebukuro	Akagiya Playguide (03) 3981-0052
	Ticket Saison (Jingu only) (03) 3981-0111
Ginza	Playguide Honten (03) 3561-8821
	Kyukyodo Ticket Service (03) 3571-0401
	Matsuya Playguide (03) 3567-8888
Tokyo	Kokusai Kanko Play Service (03) 3215-1181
	Tetsudo Kaikan Playguide (03) 3212-2443
Akasaka	Spo-nichi Ticket Center (03) 3588-5018
Ueno	Ueno AB Playguide (03) 3833-3111
	Matsuya Ticket Bureau (03) 3833-1011

Tickets for YOKOHAMA STADIUM

Yokohama	Sotetsu Kanko Join Us Playguide (045) 319-2456
	Takashimaya Ticket Shop (045) 311-1251
	Sogo Playguide (045) 465-2111
	PX Orion (045) 453-6505
	Yokohama Palace (045) 453-6671
Sakuragicho	Yomiuri Playguide (045) 201-9748
Kannai	Kinko Sports (045) 662-2727
	Kanagawa Shimbun Hot Now (045) 664-6681
Yokosuka	Keihin Tourist (0468) 23-1435
Hon-atsugi	Mirodo Playguide (0462) 30-3291
Hiratsuka	Kanagawa Chuo Kotsu (0463) 21-0655

	Umeya (0463) 22-4147
Shibuya	Tokyu Ticket Center (03) 3406-1513
Akasaka	Spo-nichi Ticket Center (03) 3588-5018
all locations	Ticket Pia (03) 5237-9999

Tickets for KAWASAKI STADIUM

Kawasaki	Travel Center Eki Bldg. Kanko (044) 200-6561
Yokohama	Sotetsu Join Us (045) 319-2456
	Yokohama Palace (045) 453-6671
	KKT Yokohama Station (045) 453-5575
Sakuragicho	Yomiuri Playguide (045) 201-9748
Yokosuka	Keihin Tourist (0468) 23-1435
Ikebukuro	Ticket Saison (03) 5990-9999
Harajuku	La Folie Playguide (03) 3401-9395

Tickets for SEIBU LIONS STADIUM

Tickets are available at main stations of the Seibu railway; at Lions' Corner shops in Ikebukuro and Harajuku; at Seibu Travel in Shin-tokorozawa, Shimbashi, and Marunouchi; and at various Seibu Kanko centers.

Tickets for NAGOYA STADIUM

Chunichi Service Center   (052) 263-7282
Matsuya Playguide   (052) 251-1841
Mitsukoshi Playguide   (052) 251-4377
Marui Playguide   (052) 264-5036
Meitetsu Playguide   (052) 585-1747
Toshin Playguide   (052) 951-0312
CBC Playguide   (052) 242-1181

Tickets for FUJIIDERA STADIUM

Kintetsu Abenobashi	Buffaloes Service Center
	(06) 628-8861
Kintetsu Ue-honmachi	Buffaloes Service Center
	(06) 772-8901

Tickets for GREEN STADIUM KOBE

Hankyu Kotsusha   (06) 373-5447
Ticket Pia   (06) 363-9999
Ticket Saison   (06) 308-9999
Mizuno Osaka-ten   (06) 223-7316
Daiei Orange Ticket   (06) 376-5500
Kobe Sogo Undo Koen Kanri Center
  (078) 792-2400

Tickets for KOSHIEN STADIUM

Umeda	Hanshin Kotsusha	(06) 347-6507
Amagasaki	Hanshin Kotsusha	(06) 411-3892
Sannomiya	Hanshin Kotsusha	(078) 221-0120
Himeji	Sanyo Kotsusha	(0792) 22-5570
	Yamato Yashiki	(0792) 23-1221
Yodoyabashi	Keihan Kotsusha	(06) 203-7000
Namba	Nankai Kokusai Ryoko	(06) 641-8686

Tickets for HEIWADAI STADIUM

Tickets are available at the "green window" ticket counters of all JR Kyushu stations; at all Lawson convenience stores; and at Playguides at Tenjin Iwataya, Fukuoka Tamaya, Fukuoka Bldg., and Hakata Daimaru; and at Daiei/Uneed Ticket Corner in Daiei and Uneed stores.

Tickets for HIROSHIMA CIVIC STADIUM

Tickets are available only at the stadium or by mail.

Tickets for all-star games usually go on sale one month in advance at the ballparks where the games are to be played. Every year there are at least two all-star games, plus a junior all-star game for farm-club players. In summers when Olympic games are held, three all-star games are played.

Tickets for the Japan Series go on sale the weekend after a club clinches the pennant. Reserved-seat tickets sell out extremely fast but bleacher seats are usually available. The Japan Series, a best-of-seven contest, is scheduled over nine days, with Monday and Friday off. All games are day games.

A word to the wise for any ballgame: Japan's climate is not always conducive to enjoyable baseball. If you think Seattle and the Pacific Northwest are wet, spend a baseball season in Tokyo, Nagoya, or Osaka. In June and early July Japan has a rainy season, September is typhoon season, and in between it rains fairly regularly, so be prepared. But rainouts are not as frequent as you'd think, as the Japanese play through torrential downpours to get games in. The field has to be a swamp before play is called.

Rainouts are often played on special days kept open for makeup games. Many of these games are scheduled in September and October, often long after the pennant races have been decided. It is very easy to obtain tickets for these games, as they often have no effect on the final standings.

Don't hesitate to attend a baseball game just because you've never been to the stadium before. Get your ticket, go inside the ballpark, and you're sure to find the friendliest, most helpful ushers in the world. Just show the woman or man your ticket stub and you'll be pleasantly directed or escorted to your seat.

To know who's playing, you'll need sharp eyes to read the players' names on the backs of their uniforms. Or brush up on your *kanji* by reading players' names on the scoreboard. There are no scorecards or programs at regular ballgames. Programs are available only for all-star games, the Japan Series, and Major League tours.

If a foul ball heads your way, don't bother chasing it. Foul balls must be returned to ushers, who promptly arrive to collect them from fans who snatch balls up. Some teams give free gift coupons in return for foul balls, others don't. In any case, all foul balls must be returned. On the other hand, home-run balls are yours for the keeping.

Hunger pangs can be alleviated at the myriad of food booths that ring the stadium. As San Diego's Jack Murphy Stadium has its sushi, and San Francisco's Candlestick Park has its tofu dogs, Japanese ballparks offer the usual American fare of hamburgers, french fries, and soft drinks. Hot dogs are found as wieners on sticks. Japanese food commonly found at ballparks includes curry rice, skewered bites of chicken or meat, and bowls of noodles. Beer, soft drinks, ice cream, potato chips, peanuts, dried squid, and other snacks are sold at booths and by roving vendors who hawk their wares all game long. Whiskey, Japanese saké, and wine are found at some parks, and are usually sold in the concourse areas. For a show, order a beer from one of the jet-packet salesmen at Seibu Lions Stadium. These beer salesmen walk around the stands carrying a scuba tank-like container that shoots beer into cups through a pressurized nozzle.

Unfortunately not one stadium offers food that could actually be called delicious. This is not to say you should avoid all the food stands, but unlike many American ballparks that take great pride in their various treats, Japanese stadiums offer standard fare that is more filling than tasty. A trip across America would get you everything from sushi in California to sauerkraut in Milwaukee to the good old hot dog with mustard anywhere.

Every region in Japan has its local delicacies, many of which are found in the traditional box lunch called *o-bentō*. These regional *o-bentō* are available at many stadiums, and you can't go wrong by sampling them. Otherwise, save your yen and before or after the game stop at any of the small restaurants that ring most stadiums. Though these places may lack baseball atmosphere, you'll likely find better food at better prices than the unfortunate fare at most stadiums.

For those needing a fix of televised baseball, there's plentiful coverage in Japan. Games are televised "live" but with a twist; most games are usually joined in progress around 7:00 p.m., usually after starting at 6:00 or 6:30 p.m. Given the slow pace of Japanese baseball, you'll probably miss only an inning or so by tuning in at 7:00 p.m. But don't get too involved in the game, as television coverage of the game ends at 9:21 p.m. at the latest.

No matter if it's the bottom of the ninth, with the bases loaded, and a full count to the cleanup hitter, coverage of the game is preempted by the news or other prime-time fare (unless the network is feeling nice that night). Baseball broadcasts are in the hands of networks that value the viewers of other programs more than baseball viewers. So at 9:21 p.m. (or occasionally earlier) when the TV broadcast ends, frustrated fans scurry to their radios and tune in the last few minutes (or innings!) of the game. On the weekend and late in the season, it seems that more games are shown in their entirety, but it's nothing you should count on.

The actual coverage of the game ranks right up there with American network and cable coverage of baseball. One great feature of televised baseball in Japan is that the score is always on display in the top corner of the screen. Even if you tune in late, you can get the score immediately. Team names are usually shown on the screen abbreviated as follows:

中　Chunichi Dragons
神　Hanshin Tigers
広　Hiroshima Carp
ヤ　Yakult Swallows
洋　Yokohama Taiyo Whales
巨　Yomiuri Giants

ダ　Daiei Hawks
近　Kintetsu Buffaloes
ロ　Lotte Orions
日　Nippon Ham Fighters
オ　Orix BlueWave
西　Seibu Lions

Other innovative on-screen graphics are the pitch-location box and pitch-velocity readout. The pitch-location box, shaped like the batter's strike zone, charts the path of each pitch. The graphic helps the fan see how a pitcher mixes up his pitches for each batter. A speed gun is used to record pitch speed, which is displayed in kilometers per hour on the screen, giving you an idea whether the pitcher has good "heat." A pitch of 150 kph is roughly equivalent to 93 mph, so anything over 150 kph means that the pitcher is throwing very hard stuff. Pitching velocity is also often displayed on stadium scoreboards.

That's as technical as it gets for Japanese baseball. Computer graphics on sports coverage are at a nascent stage in Japan. The *pièce de résistance* is the first-rate camera work, particularly evident on programs that feature sports highlights, broadcast on many stations around 11:00 p.m.

One definite technical oddity is stereo broadcasting. The networks usually have two sets of broadcasters covering a game. If you fiddle with your stereo TV, you can pick up the regular announcers on the normal band and the "celebrity" announcers on the "sub" channel. Japanese entertainers often occupy these celebrity seats and blab on and on about nothing, laughing themselves silly at being on a baseball broadcast. This frivolous waste of audio is offset by the use of the "sub" channel for English-language play-by-play coverage of games.

The bilingual system broadcasts games in Tokyo and Nagoya. In Tokyo it's Giants games from the Dome on NTV, channel 4; in Nagoya, it's Chunichi games on THK, channel 1. Osaka's KTV, channel 8, used to offer the best English TV coverage of baseball in Japan; unfortunately those broadcasts were suspended after the 1990 season.

Another great broadcast feature is the postgame "hero interview," during which the star of the game is placed on an Olympics-style podium and interviewed immediately after the game. The interview is broadcast simultaneously over the PA, so fans in the stadium can listen in. In-depth details of the game are reported in the newspapers the following morning.

Newspaper coverage of Japanese baseball is extensive, not just in regular papers but also in daily sports newspapers. The newspapers are generally fair in their coverage, though the Yomiuri publications trumpet the Giants and the Chunichi press promotes the Dragons. Of course, the regular daily newspapers' main emphasis is still news, with sports coverage amounting to two or three pages.

A few pages is not enough for hard-core sports fans, and sports dailies fill the gap. The daily sports papers are little more than scandal sheets that combine titillation (soft-core pornographic pictures and stories) with sports news. The competition among the sports papers is intense, and nothing livens things up like a good scandal or controversy.

With their bold headlines, jazzy style, color photos, and sensational stories, these sports newspapers have circulations of over one and a half million. They are chock full of statistics to delight any sabermetrician (baseball-statistics nut). Records of batting averages with runners in scoring position, how certain batters hit against certain pitchers, pitchers' strikeout records, hits allowed, and walks per nine innings are all there to feed the statistics sharks. But it is the scandals that are the meat and potatoes of the sports dailies. The minutest details of a player's, manager's, or official's life can be exploited in these papers. With Japan's extremely liberal libel laws, anything goes. These papers feed on rumors (and occasionally the truth) to provide the public what it wants—entertainment.

Any tiff or perceived tiff between a player and his manager will be played up to the hilt. Like Americans who crave details of movie stars' lives, Japanese businessmen crave baseball gossip. Sports heroes are the larger-than-life creatures in Japanese society. The sports dailies feed the frustrated Japanese male his daily dose of vicarious thrills.

The best aspect of baseball coverage in Japanese newspapers is the box score. Each batter's current home-run total and batting average is noted next to his times at bat, runs, and hits for the day's game. In contrast, *The Japan Times,* the largest of the English-language dailies, provides only line scores for games. Moreover, coverage of Japanese baseball is often less than that devoted to Major League games.

Besides *The Japan Times,* English-language dailies in Japan include *The Daily Yomiuri, Mainichi Daily News,* and *Asahi Evening News. The Japan Times* has regular in-depth articles on players and a weekly baseball columnist; *The Daily Yomiuri* has the best previews of the upcoming season and the Japan Series. The other two papers cannot compete with these two heavyweights.

These newspapers are your best source for information about upcoming games, with starting times and venues regularly listed. During the last week of a month, *The Japan Times* prints up the next month's schedule in full, essential information for stadium-hopping fans.

If you want more details on the teams and players, there's very little in English other than Wayne Graczyk's annual *Japan Pro Baseball Fan Handbook & Media Guide,* which gives complete lineups, plus batting and pitching statistics for the previous season. The book also includes a complete statistical record of all the foreign players who have played in Japan.

The Japanese press publishes numerous baseball magazines loaded with articles about players, coaches, and owners. Player portraits list the usual things like height, weight, and batting average but also include information like home address, blood type, hobbies, preferences in cars, and preferences in women (single guys' opinions only). Issues previewing the baseball season come out in late February.